A BEGINNER'S (
THE FACEl
MARKETPLACE

Learn How to Increase Your
Chances of Making a Sale

Jeff Murray

The author, Jeff Murray, originates from Fairbanks, Alaska and currently resides in Columbia, South Carolina. He first started his entrepreneurial journey in 2014. His passions include enjoying fishing, fitness, and most of all technology in his off time.

Through years of research and experience in Facebook Marketing, Jeff has generated countless sales for his business, using the methods explained in this book. He knows the struggle is real, and he also wants to help other businesses by sharing his expertise and passion for Facebook Marketing.

What he had learned took him years to achieve. This is why he would like to share his knowledge about achieving sales and customers through Facebook with others.

Disclaimer Notice:

CHAPTER ONE

INTRODUCTION TO FACEBOOK PLATFORM

Facebook, founded in 2004 by Mark Zuckerberg and his fellow Harvard University students, is a social media platform that has revolutionized the way we connect and share with others. From its humble beginnings, Facebook has grown into a global phenomenon with billions of users worldwide. In this chapter, we will explore the evolution of Facebook and how it has become a versatile platform for personal and business use.

When Facebook first launched, it was initially limited to Harvard University students. However, its popularity quickly spread to other universities, prompting the expansion of its user base. In 2006, Facebook opened its doors to the general public, allowing anyone with a valid email address to create an account. This move marked a turning point for Facebook, as it began to attract users from all walks of life.

The success of Facebook can be attributed to its user-friendly interface and innovative features. At its core, Facebook provides a space for individuals to connect with friends, family, and acquaintances. Users can create personal profiles where they can share information about themselves, post updates, and upload photos and videos. These profiles serve as a virtual representation of individuals on the platform, allowing them to express their personalities and connect with others.

One of the most prominent features of Facebook is the News Feed. The News Feed acts as a central hub where users can see updates from their friends, pages they follow, and groups they are a part of. It provides a curated stream of content that is tailored to each user's interests and preferences, allowing them to stay informed and engaged.

In addition to personal profiles, Facebook offers various tools for businesses and organizations. Pages, for instance, allow businesses to create a public presence on the platform. Businesses can share updates, post content, and engage with their audience through comments, likes, and shares. Pages provide a means for businesses to build a community, raise awareness about their products or services, and ultimately drive sales.

Facebook also offers groups, which are communities centered around specific interests or topics. Users can join groups related to their hobbies, professional interests, or local communities. Within these groups, members can engage in discussions, share resources, and connect with like-minded individuals. Groups provide a sense of belonging and foster meaningful interactions among users.

Another notable feature of Facebook is Messenger, an integrated messaging platform. Messenger allows users to have private conversations with their contacts, making it easy to stay in touch with friends and family. It has evolved beyond simple text messaging and now supports voice and video calls, as well as various interactive features like stickers and emojis.

Over the years, Facebook has continued to innovate and introduce new features. It has acquired popular platforms like Instagram and WhatsApp, expanding its reach and influence. Through strategic partnerships and investments, Facebook has positioned itself as a leader in the social media landscape.

Today, Facebook remains a powerhouse in the realm of marketing and business. Its vast user base, advanced targeting options, and advertising tools make it an attractive platform for businesses of all sizes. Whether you're a small local business or a multinational corporation, Facebook offers the tools and resources to connect with your target audience and drive results.

In conclusion, Facebook has transformed the way we connect and share with others. From its humble beginnings as a platform for Harvard students, it has grown into a global phenomenon. With its user-friendly interface, innovative features, and extensive reach, Facebook has become a versatile platform for personal connections, community building, and business growth.

COMMON FACEBOOK FEATURES

Facebook offers a variety of features that enhance communication, content sharing, and engagement among users. Let's explore some of the common features that make Facebook a dynamic and interactive platform.

News Feed:

At the heart of Facebook is the News Feed, a central hub where users can find updates from their friends, pages they follow, and groups they are a part of. The News Feed utilizes algorithms to curate a personalized stream of content tailored to each user's preferences and interests. It enables users to stay connected and informed about the latest updates from their social network.

Profile:

Every Facebook user has a personal profile, which serves as their virtual space on the platform. The profile allows users to share information about themselves, such as their bio, education, work history, and relationship status. Users can also upload photos and videos, write posts, and express their thoughts and experiences. The profile acts as a digital representation of an individual's identity on Facebook and provides a platform for self-expression and personal branding.

Friends:

Facebook revolves around the concept of connecting and interacting with others. Users can send friend requests to individuals they know or want to connect with. Upon acceptance, they become friends on the platform, enabling them to view each other's profiles, share updates, and engage in conversations. Facebook fosters social connections and enables users to maintain and strengthen relationships with their friends, both offline and online.

Groups:

Facebook Groups provide a space for users to join communities based on shared interests, hobbies, or causes. Users can find and join existing groups or create their own, inviting others to participate. Within groups, members can engage in discussions, share resources, ask questions, and organize events. Groups foster a sense of belonging, enabling users to connect with like-minded individuals, exchange knowledge, and build meaningful relationships around common interests.

Pages:

Facebook Pages are dedicated spaces for businesses, organizations, public figures, and brands to engage with their audience and share updates. Pages allow businesses to create an online presence, build a community of followers, and promote their products or services. Page administrators can post content, respond to comments, run ads, and analyze insights to understand their audience better. Facebook Pages offer powerful tools for businesses to establish their brand identity, reach a wider audience, and drive engagement and conversions.

Messenger:

Facebook Messenger is an integrated messaging platform that allows users to have private conversations with their contacts. Messenger supports text messaging, voice and video calls, file sharing, and interactive features like stickers and emojis. It provides a convenient and seamless way for users to communicate in real time, whether they are connecting with friends, family, or business contacts. Messenger enhances personal connections and enables users to stay connected and engaged beyond the public News Feed.

These common features of Facebook form the foundation of the platform's interactivity and engagement. They facilitate communication, content sharing, and community building, making Facebook a vibrant and dynamic social media platform.

A SHORT HISTORY OF FACEBOOK

Facebook's history is a remarkable tale of growth, innovation, and adaptation. From its humble beginnings as an exclusive platform for Harvard students to its current status as a global social media powerhouse, Facebook has transformed the way we connect and share with others. Let's delve into the key milestones that have shaped Facebook's journey.

In 2004, Mark Zuckerberg, along with his fellow Harvard University students, launched "Thefacebook" as a social networking platform exclusively for Harvard students. The initial concept aimed to create a digital community where students could connect with each other, share information, and build relationships within the university.

The platform quickly gained popularity, leading to its expansion beyond Harvard. It extended its reach to other prestigious universities, including Stanford, Columbia, and Yale. As Facebook expanded its user base, it became evident that its potential extended far beyond the confines of the academic sphere.

In 2006, Facebook took a significant leap forward by opening its doors to the general public. This pivotal moment marked a major turning point in the platform's history, as it allowed anyone with a valid email address to join and create a Facebook account. This decision unleashed the true power of Facebook, propelling it toward becoming a global phenomenon.

The years following its public launch saw exponential growth for Facebook. It rapidly acquired millions of users, transforming social interactions and revolutionizing the way people connect and communicate online. Facebook's user-friendly interface, intuitive features, and emphasis on connecting with friends and family attracted users from all walks of life.

In 2012, Facebook made a monumental move by acquiring Instagram, a popular photo-sharing platform. This strategic acquisition allowed Facebook to tap into the rising trend of visual content and expand its user base further. Instagram's integration with Facebook provided users with seamless cross-platform sharing and enhanced their overall experience.

In 2014, Facebook made another significant acquisition by purchasing WhatsApp, a widely used messaging application. This move strengthened Facebook's position in the mobile messaging arena and broadened its reach to an even larger audience. WhatsApp's secure and user-friendly messaging platform aligned perfectly with Facebook's vision of enabling global connectivity.

Throughout its history, Facebook has continually evolved its features and functionalities to cater to the changing needs and preferences of its users. It introduced new features such as Facebook Live, which allows users to broadcast live videos, and Marketplace, a platform for buying and selling goods within the Facebook community. These innovations have ensured that Facebook remains a dynamic and relevant platform in the ever-evolving social media landscape.

Facebook's success can also be attributed to its commitment to user privacy and security. The platform has implemented various measures to protect user data and provide users with control over their privacy settings. These efforts have been crucial in maintaining user trust and confidence in the platform.

Today, Facebook stands as the leading social media platform globally, with billions of active users worldwide. Its impact on society, communication, and business is undeniable. It has provided individuals, businesses, and organizations with a powerful tool for connecting, sharing, and engaging with others.

In conclusion, Facebook's journey from a Harvard-exclusive platform to a global social media giant is a testament to its ability to adapt, innovate, and meet the evolving needs of its users. As it continues to evolve, Facebook remains at the forefront of social connectivity, empowering individuals and businesses to forge meaningful connections in the digital age.

Why Facebook is still considered the Leading Social Media Platform for Marketing and Business:

In today's ever-evolving digital landscape, Facebook continues to hold its position as the leading social media platform for marketing and business. Despite the emergence of new platforms, Facebook offers unique advantages that make it a powerful tool for businesses of all sizes.

One of the key factors that contribute to Facebook's dominance is its unparalleled reach. With over 2.9 billion monthly active users as of April 2023 (a), Facebook provides businesses with access to a vast and diverse audience. This massive user base translates into a potential customer pool that is unparalleled on any other social media platform. Whether you're targeting a local audience or expanding your reach globally, Facebook's extensive user base ensures that your marketing efforts can reach a wide range of potential customers.

Facebook's advertising capabilities also set it apart from its competitors. The platform offers sophisticated targeting options that allow businesses to precisely tailor their ads to specific demographics, interests, behaviors, and locations. This level of precision ensures that your ads are shown to the most relevant audience, increasing the chances of engagement and conversion. Facebook's ad targeting features enable businesses to reach the right people at the right time, maximizing the return on investment for their marketing campaigns.

Moreover, Facebook provides businesses with a range of advertising tools and formats to suit their specific needs. Whether it's image-based ads, video ads, carousel ads, or immersive experiences like augmented reality ads, Facebook offers diverse options to showcase products and services in engaging and visually appealing ways. These advertising tools empower businesses to create compelling and interactive content that captivates their target audience.

Furthermore, Facebook's algorithmic power and potential for viral content make it an ideal platform for businesses looking to boost their brand visibility and reach. When users engage with your content through likes, comments, and shares, Facebook's algorithm rewards your posts with increased visibility, potentially exposing your brand to a wider audience. This viral potential can significantly amplify your marketing efforts and generate organic reach and engagement.

On a personal note, I have experienced firsthand the power and influence of Facebook as a platform for selling items through Facebook Marketplace. The platform provides a convenient and user-friendly interface for individuals to buy and sell products within their local communities. By utilizing the features and strategies that we will delve into later in this book, you can tap into the immense potential of Facebook Marketplace and effectively sell your items to interested buyers.

So, get ready to harness the power of Facebook as we embark on this journey together. With its unparalleled reach, sophisticated targeting options, and a vast array of advertising tools, Facebook remains the go-to platform for businesses looking to maximize their marketing efforts and drive success

UNDERSTANDING FACEBOOK MARKETPLACE

Facebook Marketplace is an online platform that enables individuals and businesses to buy and sell products within their local communities. It is a convenient marketplace within the Facebook social media platform, which allows users to browse, list, and purchase items from others in their area. Facebook Marketplace provides a range of features and benefits that make it a popular choice for buying and selling goods.

At its core, Facebook Marketplace serves as a virtual marketplace where users can discover and engage with products and services. It provides a user-friendly interface that simplifies the process of buying and selling, making it accessible to both experienced sellers and casual users. With a few simple steps, users can list their items for sale, set prices, and engage with potential buyers.

One of the key benefits of using Facebook Marketplace for businesses is the massive market reach it offers. With billions of active users on Facebook, businesses can tap into a vast audience and increase their brand exposure. This wide reach allows businesses to connect with potential customers who may not have been aware of their offerings through traditional marketing channels.

The user-friendly mobile app is another advantage of Facebook Marketplace. The app enables users to access the marketplace on their mobile devices, making it convenient and accessible on the go. This mobile-friendly approach aligns with the increasing trend of mobile commerce and ensures that users can easily browse, buy, and sell items from their smartphones or tablets.

Simplicity is key on Facebook Marketplace, as it offers a quick and straightforward posting process. Sellers can easily upload photos, add descriptions, set prices, and specify item details, streamlining the listing process. This simplicity saves time and effort for sellers, allowing them to efficiently list their products and reach potential buyers.

Facebook Marketplace also prioritizes local focus, allowing users to discover items available in their immediate vicinity. This local approach promotes community engagement and facilitates face-to-face transactions, providing a sense of trust and convenience for both buyers and sellers.

Engagement is a vital aspect of Facebook Marketplace, as it allows potential buyers to ask questions and interact with sellers directly. Through direct messaging, buyers can inquire about product details, negotiate prices, and arrange pickup or delivery. This customer engagement fosters trust and transparency, enhancing the buying experience for both parties.

Moreover, Facebook Marketplace promotes trust-based communities by incorporating user reviews and ratings. Sellers with positive reviews and high ratings build a reputation and credibility within the platform, encouraging buyers to have confidence in their transactions. This trust-based system helps users make informed decisions and fosters a safe and reliable marketplace environment.

Facebook Marketplace supports multiple photos for each listing, allowing sellers to showcase their products from various angles. High-quality visuals are crucial for attracting potential buyers and creating a compelling product presentation. With the ability to display multiple photos, sellers can provide a comprehensive view of their items, enhancing the chances of attracting interested buyers.

Another advantage of using Facebook Marketplace is the option for free listings and low fees. Unlike some e-commerce platforms that charge hefty fees, Facebook Marketplace provides a cost-effective solution for businesses to list and sell their products. This affordability makes it accessible to businesses of all sizes, including small and independent sellers.

Facebook Marketplace also offers multiple payment options, enabling buyers and sellers to choose their preferred method. From cash transactions to electronic payments, users have flexibility in completing their transactions securely and conveniently.

Finally, Facebook Marketplace offers brand exposure for businesses. By leveraging the platform, businesses can increase their visibility, expand their customer base, and potentially generate leads for their other online channels or physical stores. The exposure on Facebook Marketplace can complement a comprehensive omnichannel strategy, allowing businesses to reach customers across different touchpoints.

In summary, Facebook Marketplace is a user-friendly platform within the Facebook social media ecosystem that facilitates local buying and selling. With its simplicity, wide market reach, local focus, engagement features, and trust-based communities, Facebook Marketplace provides businesses with an effective avenue to showcase their products, engage with potential customers, and drive sales.

Facebook Marketplace provides businesses with an effective avenue to showcase their products, engage with potential customers, and drive sales. It presents a range of benefits that make it an attractive platform for businesses looking to expand their online presence and reach a local customer base.

One of the notable advantages of using Facebook Marketplace is its optimized browsing experience. Users can easily search for specific items or explore categories to discover new products. The platform's intuitive interface and search functionality enable users to find relevant listings quickly. Additionally, Facebook's algorithmic recommendations and personalized suggestions enhance the browsing experience, helping users discover items tailored to their interests and preferences.

The "Browse to Buy" feature further simplifies the purchasing process on Facebook Marketplace. When users find a product they are interested in, they can seamlessly transition to the seller's profile or business page to learn more about the brand and explore other offerings. This feature encourages users to engage further with the seller's brand and potentially make additional purchases, fostering customer loyalty and repeat business.

Customer engagement is a crucial aspect of successful marketing and selling, and Facebook Marketplace provides ample opportunities for direct interaction. Through comments, likes, and shares, buyers can express their interest in a listing and initiate conversations with sellers. This engagement enables sellers to provide additional information, address customer inquiries, and build relationships with their target audience. By fostering these meaningful interactions, businesses can establish trust and credibility, increasing the likelihood of successful transactions.

Trust-based communities are an essential component of Facebook Marketplace. Users have the option to join or create groups centered around specific interests or product categories. These communities create a sense of belonging and enable like-minded individuals to connect, share insights, and engage in buying and selling activities. By participating in these communities, businesses can tap into niche markets, target specific demographics, and establish themselves as trusted authorities within their respective industries.

Facebook Marketplace also supports the inclusion of multiple photos for each listing, allowing sellers to showcase their products from various angles and highlight key features. High-quality visuals play a pivotal role in capturing the attention of potential buyers and conveying the value of a product. By presenting multiple photos, sellers can provide a comprehensive and visually appealing representation of their offerings, leading to increased interest and higher conversion rates.

The quick posting process on Facebook Marketplace is a significant advantage for businesses looking to list their products efficiently. Sellers can easily create listings, add details, and publish them in a matter of minutes. This streamlined process saves time and eliminates complexities, enabling businesses to focus on other aspects of their operations.

Moreover, Facebook Marketplace offers the convenience of direct messaging, allowing buyers and sellers to communicate privately and negotiate the terms of their transactions. This feature facilitates seamless communication and enables both parties to discuss payment methods, arrange for pick-up or delivery, and address any concerns or questions. The direct messaging feature enhances the overall buying experience and promotes trust between buyers and sellers.

One of the most appealing aspects of Facebook Marketplace for businesses is the availability of free listings and low fees. Unlike some e-commerce platforms that charge significant fees for listing and selling products, Facebook Marketplace offers a cost-effective solution. Sellers can list their items without incurring upfront costs, making it an accessible platform for businesses of all sizes, including small enterprises and independent sellers.

The massive market presence of Facebook Marketplace cannot be overstated. With billions of active users, the platform provides businesses with access to a vast pool of potential customers. This expansive reach ensures that businesses can significantly expand their brand exposure and increase the chances of connecting with interested buyers.

Furthermore, Facebook Marketplace supports multiple payment options, giving users flexibility in completing their transactions. Buyers and sellers can choose from various payment methods, including cash on delivery, electronic transfers, or utilizing integrated payment systems. This versatility accommodates different preferences and fosters a seamless and secure transaction process.

In conclusion, Facebook Marketplace offers businesses a user-friendly, local-focused, and highly engaged platform to showcase their products and reach potential customers. With its optimized browsing experience, customer engagement features, trust-based communities, multiple photos, quick posting process, direct messaging, cost-effectiveness, massive market presence, and diverse payment options, Facebook Marketplace remains a leading social media platform for marketing and business.

What is FB Marketplace?

Facebook Marketplace is an online platform within the Facebook social media network that allows users to buy and sell items in their local communities. It is a convenient and accessible platform where individuals and businesses can list their products or services for sale. Users can browse through various categories, search for specific items, and connect with sellers directly through Facebook Messenger.

Facebook Marketplace is designed to be user-friendly, with a straightforward interface that is easy to navigate. It offers a dedicated mobile app, allowing users to access the marketplace on their smartphones and tablets, making it convenient for both buyers and sellers to engage in transactions anytime and anywhere.

Benefits for Businesses

Facebook Marketplace offers several benefits for businesses looking to expand their reach and increase sales:

1. **User-friendly mobile app**: With a dedicated mobile app, businesses can easily manage their listings, respond to customer inquiries, and complete transactions on the go.

2. **Simple posting**: Listing products on Facebook Marketplace is a seamless process. Businesses can quickly create appealing listings and add descriptions, prices, and images, making it easy for potential customers to discover and engage with their products.

3. **Local focus**: Facebook Marketplace emphasizes local transactions, allowing businesses to connect with buyers in their immediate vicinity. This local focus enables faster and more convenient pick-up or delivery options, appealing to customers seeking immediate solutions.

4. **Optimized browsing**: The platform provides users with a streamlined browsing experience. They can search for specific products or explore categories, and Facebook's algorithmic recommendations ensure that users discover relevant listings tailored to their interests.

5. **"Browse to Buy" feature**: The "Browse to Buy" feature enables users to seamlessly transition from browsing to exploring the seller's profile or business page. This feature encourages users to engage further with the brand and potentially make

additional purchases, fostering customer loyalty.

6. **Customer engagement**: Facebook Marketplace facilitates direct customer engagement through comments, likes, and shares. Businesses can interact with potential buyers, provide additional information, address inquiries, and build relationships, enhancing the overall buying experience.

7. **Trust-based communities**: Users can join or create groups centered around specific interests or product categories. These communities foster trust and enable businesses to target niche markets, connect with like-minded individuals, and establish themselves as trusted authorities within their industries.

8. **Support of multiple photos**: Businesses can showcase their products with multiple photos,

highlighting different angles and features. High-quality visuals play a vital role in capturing the attention of potential buyers and conveying the value of a product effectively.

9. **Quick posting process**: Facebook Marketplace offers a straightforward and efficient listing process, saving businesses time and effort. Sellers can create listings, add details, and publish them in a matter of minutes, enabling them to focus on other critical aspects of their operations.

10. **Direct messaging**: The platform's direct messaging feature allows buyers and sellers to communicate privately, negotiate terms, and address any concerns or questions. This feature enhances the overall buying experience and promotes trust between parties.

11. **Free listings and low fees**: Unlike some e-commerce platforms,

Facebook Marketplace offers free listings, making it accessible for businesses of all sizes. Additionally, the platform charges low fees, making it a cost-effective solution for businesses to showcase and sell their products.

12. **Massive market**: With billions of active users, Facebook Marketplace provides businesses with access to a vast market of potential customers. This extensive reach significantly expands brand exposure and increases the likelihood of connecting with interested buyers.

13. **Multiple payment options**: Facebook Marketplace supports various payment options, allowing users to choose their preferred method. Whether it's cash on delivery, electronic transfers, or integrated payment systems, the platform offers flexibility to accommodate different customer preferences.

14. **Brand exposure**: By utilizing Facebook Marketplace, businesses can increase their brand exposure within their local communities. The platform enables them to reach potential customers who might not have been aware of their brand through traditional marketing channels.

Overall, Facebook Marketplace provides businesses with a user-friendly, localized, and cost-effective platform to sell their products or services. Its various features and benefits make it an attractive option for businesses looking to tap into a vast user base, engage with customers, and expand their market presence.

THE POWER OF FACEBOOK MARKETPLACE

Facebook Marketplace presents a powerful opportunity for businesses to reach a wide audience and engage with potential customers in a meaningful way. With its extensive user base and robust features, Facebook Marketplace offers several advantages for businesses looking to expand their reach and drive sales.

Case Study: FB Marketplace & Meaningful Engagement

Numerous success stories demonstrate the potential of Facebook Marketplace for businesses. For example, a small boutique clothing store used Facebook Marketplace to showcase their unique products and reach a larger customer base. By leveraging the platform's user-friendly interface and optimized browsing experience, they attracted new customers, increased sales, and fostered meaningful engagement with their target audience. The direct messaging feature allowed them to address customer inquiries promptly, build relationships, and provide personalized assistance, leading to enhanced customer satisfaction and repeat business.

Relevant Statistics

Statistics further illustrate the power of Facebook Marketplace for business:

1. Facebook had 2.989 billion monthly active users in April 2023, making it the world's most active social media platform (a).

2. The total number of people using Facebook each month increased by roughly 26 million (+0.9%) in the three months leading up to April 2023 (a).

3. Facebook Marketplace is available in over 100 countries, providing businesses with a global reach (b).

4. Approximately 800 million people globally use Facebook Marketplace every month to buy and sell items (c).

5. According to Facebook, no fewer than 1.1 billion people in the US use Facebook Marketplace monthly (d).

6. Facebook Marketplace is especially popular among younger demographics, with 50% of users being under the age of 34 (e).

These statistics demonstrate the massive potential audience and engagement opportunities available on Facebook Marketplace.

Pros, Cons, and Fees of FB Marketplace

While Facebook Marketplace offers many benefits, it's important to consider both its pros and cons:

Pros:

1. ***Wide Reach:*** With billions of active users, Facebook Marketplace provides

businesses with access to a vast audience, increasing brand exposure and potential customer reach.

Facebook Marketplace offers businesses an exceptional advantage with its wide reach, providing them with access to billions of active users. This vast audience creates an unparalleled opportunity for businesses to expand their brand exposure and increase their potential customer reach.

By leveraging Facebook's extensive user base, businesses can tap into diverse demographics that span different age groups, geographical locations, and interests. This broad user base ensures that businesses can connect with a wide range of potential customers, enabling them to reach individuals who may not have been accessible through other marketing channels.

The sheer size of the Facebook Marketplace user community also means that businesses have the opportunity to connect with customers on a global scale. Whether a business is local, regional, or international in nature, Facebook Marketplace allows them to extend their reach beyond traditional boundaries, expanding their customer base across borders and time zones.

Furthermore, Facebook's powerful targeting capabilities enable businesses to optimize their reach by tailoring their marketing efforts to specific demographics, interests, and behaviors. This means that businesses can effectively deliver their products or services to the most relevant and engaged audience, maximizing their chances of converting leads into actual customers.

In addition to its vast user base, Facebook Marketplace benefits from the social nature of the platform. Users on Facebook can easily share, like, and comment on Marketplace listings, creating a ripple effect that can amplify a business's brand exposure exponentially. When users engage with a business's listing or recommend it to their friends and connections, it helps spread awareness and generate buzz, leading to increased visibility and potential customer reach.

Another advantage of Facebook Marketplace's wide reach is the opportunity it creates for businesses to tap into the growing trend of mobile commerce. With the majority of Facebook users accessing the platform through their mobile devices, businesses can connect with potential customers wherever they are, making it more convenient for users to discover, browse, and purchase products or services on the go.

Overall, the wide reach of
Facebook Marketplace presents
businesses with an unparalleled
opportunity to expand their brand
exposure and increase their potential
customer reach. By leveraging
Facebook's vast user base, powerful
targeting capabilities, and social
nature, businesses can connect with a
diverse global audience, optimize
their marketing efforts, and tap into
the growing trend of mobile
commerce.

2. **Meaningful Engagement:** The
   platform facilitates direct interaction
   between businesses and customers
   through comments, messages, and
   groups, enabling personalized
   communication and relationship-
   building.

3.   **Local Focus:** Facebook Marketplace emphasizes local transactions, making it ideal for businesses targeting customers within a specific area. This focus allows for convenient pick-up or delivery options, fostering trust and encouraging local commerce.

By prioritizing local transactions, Facebook Marketplace aligns with the growing trend of supporting local businesses and buying locally. This focus creates a sense of community and encourages users to discover and support businesses in their own neighborhoods. For businesses targeting a specific area, this localized approach presents a unique opportunity to connect with customers who are actively seeking local products and services.

The emphasis on local transactions also facilitates convenient pick-up or delivery options. Businesses can offer customers the choice to either pick up their purchases directly or arrange for local delivery. This flexibility caters to the preferences and needs of customers, allowing them to select the most convenient method of receiving their items. It also reduces the barriers to purchase, as customers can easily access products or services without lengthy shipping times or expensive delivery fees.

Furthermore, the local focus on Facebook Marketplace fosters a sense of trust and familiarity. Users often feel more comfortable engaging with businesses located in their community, as it offers a level of transparency and accountability. Customers can verify the legitimacy of a business by checking its local presence and interacting with other community members who may have had previous experiences with the business. This local validation helps build trust and confidence, increasing the likelihood of customers choosing to transact with local businesses on Facebook Marketplace.

The local focus of Facebook Marketplace also encourages and supports local commerce. It provides a platform for small and medium-sized businesses to showcase their products or services to a targeted local audience. By connecting with customers in their immediate vicinity, businesses can cultivate relationships, build a loyal customer base, and establish a strong presence within their community. Additionally, the local commerce focus fosters economic growth within the community, as transactions made through Facebook Marketplace contribute to the local economy and support local entrepreneurship.

Facebook Marketplace further enhances the local focus through its integration with Facebook Groups and Events. Businesses can join or create local groups and events to connect with potential customers who share a common location or interest. These groups and events serve as additional avenues for businesses to promote their offerings, engage with the local community, and foster a sense of belonging.

In conclusion, the local focus of Facebook Marketplace provides businesses with a platform to target customers within a specific area. The emphasis on local transactions enables convenient pick-up or delivery options, fosters trust and familiarity, and encourages local commerce. By leveraging the local community aspect, businesses can establish themselves as trusted local providers, connect with customers seeking local products or services, and contribute to the growth and vibrancy of their community's economy.

4. **Cost-Effectiveness**: Facebook Marketplace offers free listings, reducing upfront costs for businesses. Additionally, its low fees make it an affordable option for reaching a wide audience.

    Facebook Marketplace stands out as a cost-effective platform for businesses, providing them with opportunities to reduce upfront costs and reach a wide audience at affordable rates. This cost-effectiveness stems from free listings and low fees, making it an attractive option for businesses looking to maximize their budget.

Firstly, Facebook Marketplace offers businesses the advantage of free listings. Unlike traditional advertising methods or e-commerce platforms that may charge fees for listing products or services, Facebook Marketplace allows businesses to showcase their offerings without any upfront costs. This feature is particularly beneficial for small businesses or startups with limited marketing budgets, as they can promote their products or services to a vast audience without incurring additional expenses.

Moreover, Facebook Marketplace's low fees contribute to its cost-effectiveness. While the platform does charge fees for certain transactions, such as for vehicles or real estate, these fees are generally lower compared to other e-commerce platforms or online marketplaces. This affordability makes Facebook

Marketplace an attractive option for businesses of all sizes, as they can reach a wide audience and potentially generate sales without breaking the bank.

The combination of free listings and low fees on Facebook Marketplace enables businesses to allocate their marketing budget more efficiently. With reduced upfront costs, businesses can invest their resources in other areas, such as product development, customer service, or targeted advertising campaigns. This cost-saving aspect allows businesses to experiment with different strategies and optimize their marketing efforts without incurring significant financial risks.

Furthermore, the affordability of Facebook Marketplace extends to its advertising options. The platform offers businesses various advertising tools, such as boosted listings or targeted ads, which allow them to amplify their reach and target specific audiences. Compared to traditional advertising channels, such as print media or television, Facebook Marketplace advertising typically offers more cost-effective options with customizable budgets and targeting capabilities. This affordability empowers businesses to tailor their advertising spend to their specific goals and audience, ensuring that they get the most value for their investment.

The cost-effectiveness of Facebook Marketplace is particularly advantageous for businesses seeking to reach a wide audience without spending exorbitant amounts on marketing. With billions of active users, the platform offers businesses access to a vast pool of potential customers at a fraction of the cost of traditional marketing channels. This affordability, combined with the platform's wide reach, ensures that businesses can maximize their brand exposure and potential customer reach within their budgetary constraints.

In conclusion, Facebook Marketplace's cost-effectiveness is evident through its free listings, low fees, and affordable advertising options. By offering businesses the opportunity to showcase their offerings without upfront costs and reach a wide audience at affordable rates, the platform allows businesses to optimize their marketing budget, allocate resources efficiently, and potentially generate sales without excessive financial burden.

Cons:

1. Competition: As a popular platform, businesses face competition from other sellers, potentially making it harder to stand out among the crowd.

    While Facebook Marketplace offers numerous advantages for businesses, it is important to consider some potential drawbacks. One significant challenge that businesses may encounter on the platform is the high level of competition. As a popular platform with a large user base, businesses face the reality of competing with numerous other sellers, making it harder to stand out and capture the attention of potential customers.

    The popularity of Facebook Marketplace means that there are countless businesses and individuals listing their products or services, creating a crowded marketplace. This saturation of listings across various categories can make it challenging for businesses to differentiate themselves and grab the attention of their target audience. Standing out amidst the competition requires businesses to develop unique selling propositions, compelling product descriptions, eye-catching visuals, and effective marketing strategies to capture the interest of potential customers.

Moreover, the presence of numerous sellers offering similar products or services in the same geographic area can lead to price competition. Price-conscious customers may compare listings and opt for the lowest-priced option, putting pressure on businesses to lower their prices to remain competitive. This price-driven competition can affect profit margins and make it more difficult for businesses to achieve their desired profitability.

In addition to competition within the platform, businesses must also contend with external competition from other e-commerce platforms and marketplaces. While Facebook Marketplace provides access to a vast user base, businesses may need to explore additional channels to reach customers who may not be actively using the platform. This requires businesses to develop a comprehensive multi-channel marketing strategy to expand their reach and target customers across different platforms and marketplaces.

To overcome the challenges of competition on Facebook Marketplace, businesses can employ several strategies. First, businesses should focus on developing a strong brand identity and value proposition to differentiate themselves from competitors. By clearly communicating the unique benefits and values they offer, businesses can capture the attention and loyalty of potential customers.

Second, businesses can leverage Facebook's advertising tools to increase visibility and reach a more targeted audience. By strategically investing in boosted listings, targeted ads, or sponsored posts, businesses can enhance their chances of standing out in a crowded marketplace and reaching their ideal customers.

Additionally, businesses can improve their chances of success by optimizing their product listings. This includes using high-quality images, writing compelling descriptions, and providing accurate and detailed information about their products or services. By offering a seamless and positive customer experience, businesses can build trust and loyalty, making it more likely for customers to choose their listings over competitors'.

Lastly, businesses can consider exploring niche markets or targeting specific segments of the Facebook Marketplace user base. By identifying unique customer segments and tailoring their offerings to their specific needs and interests, businesses can carve out a specialized market for themselves and reduce direct competition.

In summary, while the popularity of Facebook Marketplace offers businesses access to a large user base, it also presents challenges in terms of competition. To overcome these challenges, businesses must focus on differentiation, employ effective marketing strategies, optimize their product listings, and consider targeting niche markets. By doing so, businesses can increase their chances of standing out and achieving success in a crowded marketplace.

2. Limited Categorization: Facebook Marketplace has specific product categories, which may not encompass all types of businesses or products.

While Facebook Marketplace offers a convenient platform for businesses to sell their products or services, one limitation is its limited categorization system. The platform provides specific product categories that may not encompass all types of businesses or products, potentially posing challenges for businesses looking to list their offerings accurately.

The predefined categories on Facebook Marketplace are designed to cover a wide range of commonly sold items, such as clothing, electronics, furniture, and vehicles. However, businesses offering specialized or niche products may find it challenging to fit their offerings into the available categories. This limitation can result in businesses either choosing a category that is not an exact match for their products or attempting to fit their offerings into a broader category that may not accurately represent their niche.

Consequently, the limited categorization can lead to a mismatch between the product and the category, making it more challenging for potential customers to discover specific items they are looking for. Customers browsing the platform might rely on category filters to narrow down their search, and if a product is not listed under the appropriate category, it may not appear in relevant search results, reducing its visibility.

Another consequence of limited categorization is the potential for increased competition within specific categories. If businesses are forced to choose a broader category that includes a wide range of products, they may face higher competition from other sellers who are also listed under the same category. This increased competition can make it more difficult for businesses to stand out and attract the attention of potential customers.

To address the limitation of limited categorization on Facebook Marketplace, businesses can employ several strategies. First, businesses can optimize their product listings by providing detailed and accurate descriptions, using relevant keywords, and including specific information that helps potential customers find their products. By providing clear and specific details, businesses can increase the chances of their products appearing in relevant searches, even if they are listed under a broader category.

Additionally, businesses can utilize Facebook Marketplace's "Attributes" feature. This feature allows sellers to provide additional details about their products beyond the predefined categories. By selecting relevant attributes or adding custom attributes, businesses can provide more specific information about their offerings, making it easier for potential customers to find them.

Furthermore, businesses can leverage the power of visual content by using high-quality images to showcase their products. Clear and compelling visuals can attract the attention of potential customers and overcome the limitations of categorization by capturing their interest regardless of the category in which the product is listed.

Lastly, businesses should consider supplementing their presence on Facebook Marketplace with other online platforms or their own e-commerce websites. By diversifying their online presence, businesses can ensure that they have greater control over categorization and product listing accuracy, as well as reach customers who may not actively use Facebook Marketplace.

In summary, while Facebook Marketplace offers a convenient platform for businesses to sell their products or services, the limited categorization system can pose challenges for businesses with specialized or niche offerings. To overcome these challenges, businesses can optimize their product listings, utilize attributes, focus on visual content, and explore other online platforms. By employing these strategies, businesses can mitigate the limitations of categorization and increase their visibility and chances of success on Facebook Marketplace.

3. Limited Payment Protection: While Facebook provides guidelines for safe transactions, there is a level of trust involved in transactions, and the platform does not offer robust payment protection compared to dedicated e-commerce platforms.

When conducting transactions on Facebook Marketplace, one limitation to consider is the limited payment protection provided by the platform. While Facebook does offer guidelines for safe transactions, there is a level of trust involved, and the platform does not offer the same level of robust payment protection as dedicated e-commerce platforms.

Unlike dedicated e-commerce platforms that often provide built-in payment systems or escrow services, Facebook Marketplace primarily relies on users to arrange payment directly with each other. This means that businesses and customers need to determine their preferred payment methods and establish trust before completing a transaction. While this direct payment approach offers flexibility, it also introduces some level of risk, as the platform itself does not have a standardized payment protection mechanism.

The absence of a dedicated payment protection system on Facebook Marketplace means that businesses and customers need to exercise caution and take steps to ensure secure transactions. This includes verifying the identity and credibility of the other party, thoroughly reviewing product details and descriptions, and communicating clearly regarding payment terms and expectations. It is important for both parties to be vigilant and exercise due diligence when engaging in transactions on the platform.

Another consideration is that in the event of a dispute or fraudulent activity, the resolution process on Facebook Marketplace can be more complex compared to dedicated e-commerce platforms. While Facebook provides guidelines and reporting mechanisms for reporting suspicious or fraudulent behavior, the resolution of disputes often relies on cooperation and communication between the involved parties. This process may require additional effort and time to resolve issues, and the outcome may not always be favorable for all parties involved.

To mitigate the limitations of limited payment protection on

Facebook Marketplace, businesses can take certain precautions. First, it is important to establish trust and credibility by maintaining a positive reputation through transparent and reliable communication with customers. This includes promptly responding to inquiries, providing accurate product descriptions, and delivering products or services as promised.

Additionally, businesses can consider using secure payment methods that offer buyer and seller protection, such as PayPal or other trusted third-party payment platforms. By utilizing these external payment systems, businesses can provide an extra layer of security for both themselves and their customers, reducing the risk of fraudulent transactions.

Furthermore, businesses can clearly outline their refund or return policies to manage customer expectations and address any potential issues that may arise. By being transparent about the steps involved in resolving disputes or processing refunds, businesses can enhance customer trust and minimize any potential conflicts.

Lastly, businesses may also choose to diversify their online presence by utilizing other e-commerce platforms that offer more robust payment protection measures. This allows businesses to provide customers with alternative payment options and platforms that prioritize secure transactions.

In summary, while Facebook Marketplace provides a convenient platform for transactions, limited payment protection compared to dedicated e-commerce platforms is a factor to consider. To address this limitation, businesses can establish trust, utilize secure payment methods, clearly communicate policies, and consider diversifying their online presence. By taking these precautions, businesses can mitigate the risks associated with limited payment protection and enhance the overall transaction experience on Facebook Marketplace.

Fees: Facebook Marketplace offers free listings, meaning businesses can showcase their products without any upfront cost. However, the platform may charge fees for optional features like promoting listings or using specific payment processors. These fees can vary, so it's essential to review the current fee structure on the platform.

Understanding the potential, engagement, and considerations associated with Facebook Marketplace allows businesses to make informed decisions and leverage the platform effectively for their marketing and sales strategies

Who Uses Facebook Marketplace?

Understanding the typical Facebook Marketplace user is essential for businesses aiming to target their potential customer base effectively. By profiling the typical user, businesses can tailor their marketing strategies to resonate with this audience and maximize their chances of success.

According to available data and statistics, here is a profile of the typical Facebook Marketplace user:

1. Demographics: Facebook Marketplace attracts users across various demographics, including different age groups and regions. However, it has a significant user base among younger demographics, with approximately 50% of users being under the age of 34 (a).

2. Geographic Reach: Facebook Marketplace has a global presence, available in over 100 countries (b). It offers businesses the opportunity to

target local customers specifically, making it ideal for localized transactions.

3. User Base: As of the first quarter of 2021, Facebook Marketplace had over 1 billion monthly active users (c). This massive user base indicates a vast potential audience for businesses to connect with and sell their products or services to.

4. Online Shoppers: Facebook Marketplace users are actively engaged in online shopping. The platform's ease of use, local focus, and the ability to discover unique items attract users seeking both new and second-hand goods (d).

5. Mobile Users: Mobile usage is prevalent among Facebook Marketplace users, as the platform is accessible through the Facebook mobile app. This mobile-friendly approach allows users to browse and

buy items conveniently on their smartphones or tablets.

Understanding these user demographics and behaviors can help businesses tailor their listings, advertisements, and customer engagement strategies to effectively reach and engage with their target audience on Facebook Marketplace.

Chapter Summary and Key Takeaways:

In this chapter, we explored the concept of Facebook Marketplace and its potential for businesses. We discussed the user-friendly features of the platform, its benefits for business, and its wide reach. Additionally, we examined the power of Facebook Marketplace in fostering meaningful engagement and highlighted relevant statistics that demonstrate its popularity among users.

Key Takeaways:

1. Facebook Marketplace offers a user-friendly platform for businesses to sell products and engage with customers.

2. The platform's features, such as optimized browsing, direct messaging, and local focus, contribute to a positive user experience.

3. Facebook Marketplace provides access to a massive user base, with billions of monthly active users worldwide.

4. Businesses can leverage Facebook Marketplace to reach their target audience, foster meaningful engagement, and drive sales.

In the next chapter, we will dive deeper into how to set up the FB Marketplace, understanding the dashboard, and personalizing the profile. Get ready to unlock the secrets to setting up the FB Marketplace!

CHAPTER TWO

SETTING UP YOUR FACEBOOK MARKETPLACE

In this chapter, we will guide you through the process of setting up your Facebook Marketplace account, understanding the dashboard, and personalizing your profile. By the end of this chapter, you'll be well-equipped to make a strong impression on potential buyers and optimize your selling experience on the platform.

Chapter Hook: Picture this: Two years ago, I found myself in a cluttered garage, surrounded by items I no longer needed. I had heard about the potential of Facebook Marketplace as a selling platform and decided to give it a try. Little did I know that this decision would be a game-changer. As I listed my first item, a vintage bicycle, I received an overwhelming response. Within a matter of days, it was sold, and I realized the power of Facebook Marketplace. Since then, I have successfully sold various items, generating over $15,000 in revenue. Let me take you on the journey of setting up your own Facebook Marketplace account, so you too can experience the joy of turning unused items into cash.

SETTING UP YOUR FACEBOOK ACCOUNT (IF NOT ALREADY DONE)

Before diving into Facebook Marketplace, you need to have a Facebook account. If you already have an account, you can skip this section. Otherwise, follow these steps to create a new Facebook account:

1. Visit the Facebook website: Open your preferred web browser and go to www.facebook.com.

2. Sign up: On the Facebook homepage, you will see a sign-up form. Fill in the required information, including your full name, email address or phone number, password, date of birth, and gender.

3. Verify your account: Facebook will send a verification code to the email address or phone number you provided. Enter the code in the verification field to confirm your account.

4. Complete your profile: After verification, Facebook will guide you through a series of steps to set up your profile. This includes adding a profile picture, finding friends, and personalizing your profile with additional information.

Setting Up Your Profile:

Once you have created your Facebook account, it's essential to set up your profile to make it engaging and reflective of your personal or business identity. Follow these steps:

1. Add a profile picture: Choose a clear and high-quality photo of yourself or your business logo. This helps others recognize you and build trust.

2. Fill out your basic information: Go to your profile, click on "About," and enter details such as your work and education history, location, and relationship status. This information can help others connect with you and understand your background.

3. Customize your profile: Facebook allows you to personalize your profile with a cover photo, featured photos, and featured sections. Add images or sections that showcase your interests, hobbies, or achievements.

Best Practices for Your Profile:

To make the most of your Facebook profile, consider these best practices:

1. Privacy settings: Review your privacy settings and choose the appropriate level of visibility for your posts and personal information. You can control who can see your posts, who can send you friend requests, and more.

2. Professionalism: If you're using Facebook for business, ensure that your profile reflects professionalism. Avoid posting controversial or inappropriate content that may harm your reputation.

3. Consistency: Maintain a consistent tone and style across your profile. Use language and imagery that align with your personal or business brand.

4. Regular updates: Keep your profile up to date with current information, such as changes in contact details, work

history, or recent achievements. This shows that you are an active and engaged user.

By following these steps and best practices, you can create a Facebook account and profile that represents you or your business accurately and professionally.

HOW TO SET UP FACEBOOK MARKETPLACE

Facebook Marketplace provides a convenient platform for buying and selling items within your local community. Follow these step-by-step instructions to activate the Marketplace feature on Facebook:

1. Accessing FB Marketplace:

   - Open the Facebook app or website.

   - On the app, tap the three horizontal lines (menu) at the

bottom right. On the website, locate the Marketplace tab on the left-hand side.

- Tap or click on the Marketplace icon.

2. Requirements:

- You must have a Facebook account in good standing that is at least 30 days old.

- Facebook Marketplace should be available in your country.

- To access the selling feature, you need to have a listed item for sale. To access the buying feature, you can browse items without listing your own.

- Adhere to the general rules set by Facebook, such as complying with their commerce policies, not selling prohibited items, and following community guidelines.

3. Selling an item:

- Tap the "Sell" button.

- Select the item category and provide a detailed description, including price, condition, and location.

- Add clear and appealing photos to attract potential buyers.

- Review your listing and click "Post" to make it visible on Marketplace.

4. Buying something:

- Browse through the categories or use the search bar to find items of interest.

- Filter results based on location, price range, and other preferences.

- Click on an item to view more details, including the seller's profile and item description.

- If interested, use the "Message" button to communicate with the seller and arrange the purchase.

5. General rules:

- Respect the terms of service and community standards provided by Facebook.

- Be honest and accurate in your listings, representing items truthfully.

- Maintain clear and timely communication with buyers or sellers.

- Follow local laws and regulations regarding the sale of specific items.

By following these steps and adhering to the guidelines, you can activate and utilize Facebook Marketplace to buy and sell items within your local community.

PERSONALIZING YOUR PROFILE FOR HIGHER VISIBILITY

Optimizing your Facebook profile and Marketplace store can significantly enhance your visibility and make a positive first impression on potential buyers. Here are some tips to personalize your profile for higher visibility:

1. Profile Picture: Choose a clear and professional-looking profile picture. It could be your own photo or a logo representing your business.

2. Cover Photo: Utilize the cover photo section to showcase your brand, products, or a visually appealing image related to your business.

3. About Section: Craft a compelling and concise "About" section that highlights key information about your business, such as what you sell, your

unique selling points, and any special offers or promotions.

4. Marketplace Store Name: Opt for a store name that is memorable and aligned with your brand. This will make it easier for customers to find you and associate your name with your products.

5. Detailed Descriptions: When listing items on Marketplace, provide thorough and accurate descriptions. Include relevant keywords, specifications, and any unique features to attract potential buyers.

6. High-Quality Photos: Use high-resolution images that showcase your products in the best possible light. Consider different angles, close-ups, and lifestyle shots to give buyers a comprehensive view.

7. Pricing Strategy: Research similar items on Marketplace to determine competitive pricing. Offering fair and

reasonable prices can attract more buyers and increase your visibility.

8. Prompt Responses: Be proactive in responding to inquiries and messages from potential buyers. Quick and friendly communication builds trust and enhances your reputation as a reliable seller.

9. Positive Reviews: Encourage satisfied customers to leave positive reviews on your profile or the Marketplace listings. Positive reviews can build credibility and influence the purchasing decisions of others.

10. Share Listings: Share your Marketplace listings on your personal Facebook timeline and other relevant groups to expand your reach and increase visibility.

By implementing these profile personalization techniques, you can enhance your visibility on Facebook Marketplace and make a lasting impression on potential buyers.

Chapter Summary: In this chapter, we discussed the process of setting up your Facebook Marketplace account, including creating a Facebook account, setting up your profile, and personalizing it for better visibility. We also provided a step-by-step guide on activating the Marketplace feature, along with tips to optimize your profile and store. Personalizing your profile and ensuring it reflects your brand identity is essential for attracting potential buyers and standing out in the marketplace.

In the next chapter, we will delve into the crucial aspects of product listing, including writing compelling descriptions, capturing high-quality product images, and implementing effective pricing strategies. These elements are key to grabbing the attention of potential buyers and maximizing your chances of making successful sales on Facebook Marketplace.

CHAPTER

THREE

LISTING ITEMS

Chapter Summary: In this chapter, we will explore the process of creating effective listings on Facebook Marketplace. We'll discuss the steps involved in creating a listing, as well as techniques to improve your listing to attract potential buyers. A well-crafted listing can significantly increase your chances of making successful sales on Facebook Marketplace.

Chapter Hook: Imagine the vast number of opportunities that arise on Facebook

Marketplace. In May 2017 alone, 18 million new items were posted for sale on the platform. With the continuous growth of Facebook Marketplace, the potential for reaching a wide audience and making successful sales has skyrocketed. Let's dive into the strategies for creating compelling listings that will help you stand out in this ever-expanding marketplace.

Creating a Listing:

1. Item Details: Provide accurate and detailed information about the item you are listing. Include the brand, model, condition, dimensions, and any other relevant specifications.

2. Compelling Title: Craft a concise and attention-grabbing title that highlights the key features or selling points of the item. Use descriptive words to attract potential buyers.

3. Descriptive Description: Write a compelling description that provides further details about the item, its

condition, usage history, and any unique characteristics. Be honest and transparent to build trust with potential buyers.

4. High-Quality Photos: Capture clear and well-lit photos that showcase the item from different angles. Use natural lighting and avoid cluttered backgrounds to ensure the item stands out.

5. Pricing: Set a competitive and reasonable price for your item. Research similar listings on Marketplace to gauge the market value and adjust your price accordingly.

6. Categorization: Choose the appropriate category and subcategory for your item. This will help potential buyers find your listing more easily when they browse through specific categories.

7. Delivery Options: Clearly specify whether you offer shipping or only local pickup. Including shipping information can expand your potential customer base, but make sure to factor in shipping costs and logistics.

Improving Your Listing:

1. Keyword Optimization: Incorporate relevant keywords in your title and description to improve the discoverability of your listing. Think about the terms potential buyers might use when searching for items like yours.

   Keyword optimization is a crucial aspect of maximizing the discoverability and visibility of your listings on platforms like Facebook Marketplace. By incorporating relevant keywords in your title and description, you can enhance the chances of potential buyers finding your products or services when they perform searches on the platform.

When optimizing your listing's keywords, it's essential to put yourself in the shoes of potential buyers and consider the terms they are likely to use when searching for items like yours. Think about the specific features, attributes, or benefits of your product or service that are most relevant to your target audience. These can include brand names, product names, sizes, colors, materials, styles, or any other distinguishing characteristics.

To start, focus on optimizing the title of your listing. This is the first element that potential buyers will see and plays a crucial role in capturing their attention. Incorporate relevant keywords that accurately describe your product or service and highlight its unique selling points. Keep the title concise, clear, and engaging, making sure to include the most important keywords that align with what buyers are searching for.

Next, optimize the description of your listing. This is an opportunity to provide more detailed information about your product or service while incorporating additional relevant keywords. Make sure to present the features, benefits, and specifications in a clear and concise manner. Use bullet points or subheadings to break down the information and make it easily scannable for potential buyers.

When selecting keywords, it's important to strike a balance between specificity and broader relevance. While specific keywords can help you target a niche audience, broader keywords can attract a wider range of potential buyers. Consider using a combination of both to optimize your listing for different search queries and increase its chances of being discovered.

Additionally, it can be helpful to conduct keyword research to identify popular search terms and phrases related to your product or service. There are various keyword research tools available that can provide insights into search volume, competition, and related keywords. By utilizing these tools, you can uncover keywords that are highly relevant to your offering and have a higher likelihood of driving traffic to your listing.

However, it's important to avoid keyword stuffing, which is the excessive and unnatural use of keywords in an attempt to manipulate search rankings. This can have a negative impact on your listing's visibility and may even result in penalties from the platform. Focus on incorporating keywords in a way that reads naturally and provides valuable information to potential buyers.

Regularly monitoring the performance of your listings and making adjustments to your keyword optimization strategy based on insights and feedback from buyers is also crucial. By analyzing which keywords are driving the most traffic and conversions, you can refine and fine-tune your keyword strategy over time to maximize the effectiveness of your listings.

In conclusion, keyword optimization is a vital component of improving the discoverability of your listings on Facebook Marketplace. By incorporating relevant keywords in your title and description, you can increase the chances of potential buyers finding your products or services when they perform searches on the platform. By striking the right balance between specificity and broader relevance and conducting keyword research, you can optimize your listings to align with what buyers are searching for and enhance your overall visibility on the platform.

2. Highlight Unique Selling Points: If your item has any special features, warranties, or accessories, highlight them in your description. This can make your listing more appealing to potential buyers.

Highlighting the unique selling points (USPs) of your products or services is a valuable strategy to make your listings more appealing to potential buyers on Facebook Marketplace. By emphasizing special features, warranties, accessories, or any other distinguishing factors, you can capture the attention of buyers and differentiate your offerings from competitors.

When crafting your listing description, it's essential to identify the specific aspects of your product or service that set it apart from similar offerings in the marketplace. These unique selling points can be the key factors that motivate potential buyers to choose your listing over others. By effectively communicating these USPs, you can create a compelling narrative that engages buyers and convinces them that your offering is the best fit for their needs.

Start by thoroughly understanding your product or service and identifying its standout features. Consider the benefits and advantages that it offers to customers and how it addresses their pain points or solves their problems. These unique features could include innovative technology, high-quality materials, exceptional durability, energy efficiency, ease of use, customization options, or any other attribute that adds value.

Once you have identified the USPs, incorporate them into your listing description. Begin by capturing the buyer's attention in the opening lines by highlighting the most compelling USPs. This can help create immediate interest and encourage potential buyers to continue reading.

As you describe your product or service, provide specific details about each unique selling point and explain how it enhances the buyer's experience. Use descriptive language and emphasize the benefits that customers will gain by choosing your offering. Whether it's a comprehensive warranty that provides peace of mind, exclusive accessories that enhance functionality, or a unique design that stands out from the crowd, clearly articulate these points to showcase the added value you are offering.

To make your listing more visually appealing, consider incorporating high-quality images that highlight unique features or accessories. Visuals can often convey the USPs more effectively than text alone, enabling potential buyers to visualize how the product or service will benefit them.

In addition to highlighting the USPs, it's important to be transparent and provide accurate information in your description. Include any relevant details about product specifications, dimensions, compatibility, or any other information that buyers may find useful when making a purchasing decision. This transparency builds trust and confidence in potential buyers, increasing the likelihood of conversions.

Regularly review and update your listings to ensure that your unique selling points are effectively communicated and remain relevant. As market trends change and new competitors enter the space, it's important to stay proactive and adapt your messaging to stay ahead.

By highlighting the unique selling points of your products or services, you can create more appealing and persuasive listings on Facebook Marketplace. Effective communication of these USPs will help you stand out from the competition, attract the attention of potential buyers, and increase the chances of successful transactions.

3. Update Availability: Regularly update your listings to indicate whether items are still available or have been sold. This helps maintain accuracy and avoids potential frustration for buyers.

Regularly updating the availability of your listings on Facebook Marketplace is crucial for maintaining accuracy, managing buyer expectations, and avoiding potential frustration. By promptly indicating whether items are still available or have been sold, you can provide a positive and reliable experience for potential buyers.

When a listing remains active on the platform even after the item has been sold, it can lead to confusion and disappointment among interested buyers. They may reach out to inquire about the availability of the product, only to discover that it is no longer accessible. This can result in wasted time and effort for both the buyer and the seller.

To ensure an optimal experience for potential buyers, it's important to update your listings as soon as an item is sold or is no longer available. This can be done in a few simple steps:

Regularly monitor your listings: Make it a habit to check your listings frequently to keep track of the availability status of each item. By staying proactive, you can promptly update the listings and avoid any potential delays or confusion.

Mark items as sold or remove the listing: Once an item is sold, you have two options. You can either mark the item as sold within the Facebook Marketplace interface, which keeps the listing visible but indicates that it is no longer available. Alternatively, you can remove the listing entirely. Choose the option that aligns with your preference and best serves the needs of potential buyers.

Communicate with interested buyers: If you receive inquiries about an item that has been sold, promptly respond and inform the interested buyer that the item is no longer available. If applicable, you can provide alternative suggestions or let them know if you have similar items that may be of interest to them.

Consistently updating the availability of your listings not only helps potential buyers make informed decisions but also reflects positively on your reputation as a seller. It demonstrates your attentiveness, professionalism, and commitment to providing accurate information.

In addition to updating the availability status of your listings, it's also important to promptly remove or update any outdated or irrelevant listings. If an item has been listed for an extended period without any inquiries or interest, consider removing it from the platform to declutter your listings and maintain a streamlined and organized presence.

By regularly updating the availability of your listings on Facebook Marketplace, you contribute to a positive user experience, build trust with potential buyers, and increase the efficiency of your transactions.

4. Customer Reviews and Ratings: Encourage satisfied customers to leave positive reviews and ratings on your profile. Positive feedback enhances your reputation and builds trust among potential buyers.

Customer reviews and ratings play a significant role in building trust and credibility on Facebook Marketplace. Encouraging satisfied customers to leave positive reviews and ratings on your profile can have a positive impact on your reputation and attract more potential buyers to your listings.

Positive reviews and ratings serve as social proof, indicating to potential buyers that others have had a positive experience with your products or services. They provide valuable feedback and reassurance, helping to alleviate any concerns or doubts that potential buyers may have. Here's how you can encourage and leverage customer reviews and ratings:

Provide exceptional customer service: Delivering outstanding customer service is the foundation for obtaining positive reviews and ratings. Ensure that you go above and beyond to meet customer expectations, promptly respond to inquiries or concerns, and resolve any issues that may arise. By delivering a great experience, you increase the likelihood of customers leaving positive feedback.

Follow up with customers: After a transaction, consider following up with customers to check their satisfaction with the product or service they purchased. This gesture shows that you value their feedback and provides an opportunity to address any concerns before they escalate. If customers express satisfaction, kindly request that they consider leaving a review or rating on your profile.

Remind customers through messaging: When communicating with customers through messages on Facebook Marketplace, you can politely remind them to leave a review or rating if they had a positive experience. Keep the reminder short, appreciative, and non-intrusive. For example, you could say, "Thank you for your purchase! If you enjoyed your experience, we would greatly appreciate it if you could leave a review on our profile."

Make it easy for customers to leave reviews: Provide clear instructions on how customers can leave a review or rating on your profile. Direct them to the appropriate section of your profile or share a direct link to make the process as seamless as possible. The easier it is for customers to leave feedback, the more likely they are to do so.

Showcase positive reviews and ratings: Once you start receiving positive reviews and ratings, highlight them on your Facebook Marketplace profile or in your listing descriptions. Consider taking screenshots of positive feedback and sharing them as social proof in your marketing efforts. This can further build trust and confidence among potential buyers.

Respond to reviews: Engage with customers who leave reviews, both positive and negative. Express gratitude for positive feedback and address any concerns or issues raised in negative reviews. Responding to reviews shows that you value customer feedback and are committed to continuously improving your products or services.

It's important to note that while encouraging positive reviews is valuable, it's essential to maintain authenticity and integrity in the process. Avoid incentivizing customers to leave positive feedback or fabricating reviews, as this can harm your reputation if discovered.

By actively seeking and leveraging customer reviews and ratings, you can enhance your reputation on Facebook Marketplace, build trust among potential buyers, and increase the likelihood of successful transactions. Positive feedback serves as a powerful tool for attracting new customers and establishing a positive online presence.

By following these steps and implementing the tips provided, you can create compelling listings that capture the attention of potential buyers on Facebook Marketplace.

WHAT TO SELL AND WHAT NOT TO SELL ON FACEBOOK MARKETPLACE

Categories of Items on Facebook Marketplace: Facebook Marketplace provides a wide range of categories to accommodate various types of items. Some of the main categories include:

1. Deals: Items that are discounted or offered at a special price.

2. Clothing & Accessories: Apparel, shoes, bags, and fashion accessories.

3. Classifieds: Services, jobs, and rentals.

4. Electronics: Gadgets, computers, audiovisual equipment, and other electronic devices.

5. Entertainment: Books, movies, music, and video games.

6. Family: Baby gear, toys, and kids' clothing.

7. Hobbies: Crafts, sporting goods, instruments, and collectibles.

8. Housing: Rental properties, houses for sale, and real estate services.

9. Home & Garden: Furniture, decor, appliances, and gardening tools.

10. Vehicles: Cars, motorcycles, trucks, and other vehicles.

11. Home Sales: Houses, apartments, and condos available for purchase.

Examples of Prohibited Items: While Facebook Marketplace provides a platform to sell a wide range of items, certain products and services are not allowed due to various reasons, including legal restrictions and community standards. Some examples of items that cannot be sold on Facebook Marketplace include:

1. Adult products: Sex toys, explicit content, and adult services.

2. Alcohol: Alcoholic beverages, including homemade products.

3. Animals: Live animals, endangered species, and animal parts.

4. Body parts and fluids: Human organs, blood, or bodily fluids.

5. Digital media and electronic devices: Pirated software, hacked accounts, or devices that facilitate unauthorized access.

6. Documents, currency, and financial instruments: Counterfeit money, passports, IDs, or credit cards.

7. Gambling: Lottery tickets, online gambling services, or betting equipment.

8. Hazardous goods and materials: Explosives, fireworks, toxic substances, or weapons.

9. Human exploitation and sexual services: Trafficking, prostitution, or adult entertainment services.

10. Ingestible supplements: Unapproved drugs, dietary supplements, or weight loss products.

11. Jobs: Job listings or employment opportunities.

12. Medical and healthcare products: Prescription medications, medical equipment, or unapproved health supplements.

13. Products with overtly sexualized positioning: Sexually suggestive items or content.

14. Recalled products: Items subject to safety recalls or those that pose a risk to consumers.

15. Services: Personal services, such as babysitting or house cleaning.

16. Stolen goods: Items obtained through illegal means or stolen property.

17. Digital products and subscriptions: Software licenses, e-books, or digital downloads.

18. Tobacco products and related paraphernalia: Cigarettes, cigars, vaping products, or smoking accessories.

19. Weapons, ammunition, and explosives: Firearms, ammunition, explosives, or weapons parts.

CREATING A LISTING ON FACEBOOK MARKETPLACE

1. Access Facebook Marketplace: From your News Feed, click on the Marketplace icon.

2. Start a New Listing: Click on "Create a new listing" from the menu options in the Marketplace.

3. Select the Product: Choose the product or item you want to list from the available options.

4. Fill in Listing Details: On the next page, select the appropriate product category, provide a clear and concise title, describe the item accurately, set the price, and specify your location.

5. Add Photos: Upload high-quality photos of the item from different angles to showcase its condition and attract potential buyers.

6. Review and Publish: Double-check all the information you have entered, including the description and price. Once you are satisfied, click on "Publish" to make your listing visible on Facebook Marketplace.

7. Multiple Listing Locations (Optional): Facebook Marketplace allows you to list your product in more than one location, increasing its visibility to potential buyers in different areas.

THE IMPORTANCE OF PICTURES IN YOUR LISTINGS

Importance of High-Quality Photos:
High-quality photos play a vital role in grabbing the attention of potential buyers and creating a positive impression of your products. Here are a few reasons why they are important:

1. Visual Appeal: Clear, well-lit, and aesthetically pleasing images make your products more appealing to buyers, increasing their likelihood of engaging with your listings.

2. Trust and Confidence: High-quality photos build trust and confidence in buyers, as they can get a better understanding of the product's condition, quality, and features.

3. Differentiation: Well-captured images differentiate your listings from others,

making them stand out in a competitive marketplace.

4. Conversion Rates: Compelling visuals have the potential to drive higher click-through rates and conversions, leading to more successful sales.

Tips for Taking Great Product Photos: To enhance your product listings with eye-catching visuals, consider the following tips when taking product photos for Facebook Marketplace:

- Get the item camera-ready: Clean and prepare the product before capturing images.

- Fill the frame: Ensure the product occupies a significant portion of the frame, providing clear details.

- Shoot in natural light: Utilize natural lighting to showcase accurate colors and avoid harsh shadows.

- Omit other objects: Remove distractions from the background to keep the focus on the product.

- Stage the item: Present the product in an appealing setting or context to help buyers envision its use.

- Include several detailed shots: Capture close-ups and multiple angles to showcase product features.

- Don't use stock photography: Utilize original photos that accurately represent the item you are selling.

- Keep it steady: Use a tripod or stabilize your hands to avoid blurry images.

- Use photo editing software: Enhance your photos by adjusting brightness, contrast, and sharpness if needed.

CRAFTING A COMPELLING PRODUCT DESCRIPTION

Crafting a Compelling Product Description: A well-written product description can greatly influence a buyer's decision and increase the chances of a successful sale. Here are some tips and techniques to create compelling product descriptions:

1. Know your target audience: Understand your target audience's needs, preferences, and pain points to tailor your description accordingly.

2. Highlight key features and benefits: Clearly articulate the unique features and benefits of your product, emphasizing how it solves a problem or enhances the buyer's life.

3. Use persuasive language: Employ descriptive and engaging language to create an emotional connection with

potential buyers. Use words that evoke positive emotions and create a sense of urgency.

4. Keep it concise and scannable: Break down the description into paragraphs or bullet points to make it easy to read and scan. Use subheadings to highlight important information.

5. Provide specific details: Include relevant details such as dimensions, materials, colors, and any additional accessories or components included with the product.

6. Be honest and transparent: Ensure your description accurately represents the product's condition, specifications, and any potential limitations or imperfections.

7. Incorporate keywords: Use relevant keywords in your description to improve visibility in search results and attract the right audience.

8. Use social proof: If applicable, mention positive reviews, testimonials, or ratings from previous customers to build trust and credibility.

9. Include a clear call-to-action: Encourage potential buyers to take action by providing a clear call-to-action, such as "Buy Now," "Message for more details," or "Limited stock available."

PRICING YOUR ITEMS EFFECTIVELY

Pricing Your Items Effectively: Setting the right price is crucial for attracting buyers and maximizing your profits. Here are some strategies and tips for pricing your items effectively:

1. Research the market: Conduct thorough market research to

understand the pricing trends for similar products on Facebook Marketplace. Consider factors such as brand, condition, age, and demand.

2. Calculate your costs: Determine the costs associated with acquiring or producing the item, including sourcing, shipping, packaging, and any fees or commissions. Factor in your desired profit margin.

3. Consider value perception: Assess the perceived value of your product based on its quality, uniqueness, and any additional features or benefits it offers. Adjust the price accordingly.

4. Competitive analysis: Analyze your competitors' pricing strategies and position your items competitively. Consider offering competitive prices or unique selling propositions to attract buyers.

5. Bundle or upsell: Consider bundling related items together or offering

upsells to increase the overall value and justify a higher price point.

6. Seasonal pricing: Adjust your prices based on seasonal demand or fluctuations in the market. Offer discounts or promotions during slower periods to stimulate sales.

7. Test and iterate: Start with a reasonable price and monitor buyer response. If your items are not selling, consider adjusting the price gradually until you find the sweet spot.

8. Offer negotiation: Be open to negotiation but set your minimum acceptable price. Allow buyers to make offers and find a mutually beneficial price point.

9. Highlight value-add: Emphasize any additional value you provide, such as free shipping, extended warranties, or exceptional customer service, to justify a higher price.

Monitor and adjust: Continuously monitor the market and adjust your prices accordingly to stay competitive and maximize profitability.

ABOUT SHIPPING

About Shipping on Facebook Marketplace: When it comes to shipping on Facebook Marketplace, here are some key points to understand:

1. Free Shipping Eligibility: Sellers can choose to offer free shipping for their listings. Free shipping eligibility is determined by various factors, including the item's price, category, and the seller's shipping history.

2. Fees: Facebook Marketplace does not charge any listing fees. However, additional fees may apply if you choose to use shipping services

provided by Facebook, such as the prepaid shipping label option.

3. Tips for Packing and Shipping Items: Ensure that your items are appropriately packaged to prevent damage during transit. Use suitable materials, such as bubble wrap or packing peanuts, and choose sturdy boxes or envelopes. Consider adding fragile or delicate labels to ensure proper handling.

4. Prepaid Shipping Labels: Facebook Marketplace offers the option to purchase and print prepaid shipping labels directly through the platform. This feature simplifies the shipping process and provides a convenient way to track packages.

5. Tax Forms: Depending on your location and the nature of your business, you may be required to handle tax obligations related to shipping. Familiarize yourself with

relevant tax laws and consult with a tax professional if needed.

6. Shipping Performance: Maintain a good shipping performance by shipping items promptly and providing accurate tracking information. Consistently meeting buyer expectations helps build trust and positive reviews.

7. Issues Buying or Selling with Shipping: Occasionally, issues may arise with shipping, such as lost packages or items arriving in poor condition. In such cases, communicate with the buyer or seller to resolve the problem amicably. If necessary, utilize the available dispute resolution processes provided by Facebook Marketplace.

Key Takeaways:

1. Understand your audience: Before creating a listing, it's crucial to understand your target audience and tailor your description, pricing, and visuals to appeal to them specifically.

2. Accurate and detailed descriptions: Provide clear and concise descriptions of your items, including relevant details such as brand, condition, size, and any additional features. Be honest and transparent to build trust with potential buyers.

3. High-quality visuals: Include high-resolution images of your items from different angles to give potential buyers a clear idea of what they can expect. Clean and well-lit photos can significantly improve the appeal of your listings.

4. Competitive pricing: Research the market to determine a fair and competitive price for your items.

Consider factors such as condition, age, and demand to set a price that attracts buyers while ensuring a reasonable profit for yourself.

5. Effective titles and keywords: Craft attention-grabbing titles for your listings using relevant keywords that potential buyers might search for. Incorporate specific details like brand, model, or size to improve search visibility.

6. Promote unique selling points: Highlight any unique features, benefits, or value propositions of your items in the description. This helps differentiate your listing from others and increases the chances of attracting buyers.

7. Regularly update and refresh listings: Keep your listings up to date by removing sold items and adding new ones. Refreshing your listings periodically can give them more

visibility and increase the likelihood of making sales.

In the next chapter, we will delve into Marketing Techniques to Enhance Sales. We'll discuss the importance of effective communication, leveraging Facebook Ads, optimizing for search engine visibility, and utilizing social proof to build trust and credibility. So, get ready to learn the secrets of successful marketing in the next chapter!

CHAPTER FOUR

MARKETING TECHNIQUES TO ENHANCE SALES ON FACEBOOK MARKETPLACE

Chapter Summary: In this chapter, we will explore various marketing techniques to enhance sales on Facebook Marketplace. We'll discuss the importance of effective communication, leveraging Facebook Ads, optimizing for search engine visibility, and utilizing social proof to build trust and credibility.

Chapter Hook: Imagine starting out on Facebook Marketplace, excited to sell your products, but struggling to attract buyers and make sales. Jeff Murray, an experienced seller, faced similar challenges early on. However, through trial and error, he discovered unique marketing strategies that transformed his sales on Facebook Marketplace. In this chapter, we'll delve into these practical and replicable techniques, guiding you on how to effectively market your listings for improved sales.

EFFECTIVE COMMUNICATION

Effective Communication: Effective communication is crucial for engaging potential buyers and building trust. Here are some tips to enhance communication on Facebook Marketplace:

1. Prompt Responses: Respond to inquiries and messages from interested buyers in a timely manner. Quick and helpful responses show professionalism and increase the chances of successful transactions.

Prompt responses to inquiries and messages from interested buyers are crucial for maintaining professionalism and maximizing the chances of successful transactions on Facebook Marketplace. By responding in a timely and helpful manner, you demonstrate your commitment to excellent customer service and create a positive impression on potential buyers.

Here are some key reasons why prompt responses are essential:

☐ Engage potential buyers: When potential buyers reach out with inquiries or messages, they are actively expressing interest in your product or service. By responding promptly, you engage them while their interest is high, increasing the likelihood of a successful transaction. Delayed responses may lead to a loss of interest or

frustration, causing potential
buyers to seek alternatives.

☐ Build trust and credibility:
Quick and helpful responses to
inquiries and messages
establish trust and credibility
with potential buyers. It shows
that you are attentive, reliable,
and committed to providing
excellent customer service.
This trust is essential in
building a positive reputation
and encouraging potential
buyers to feel confident in their
decision to transact with you.

☐ Provide accurate information:
Responding promptly allows
you to provide accurate and up-
to-date information to potential
buyers. They may have specific
questions about the product, its
features, pricing, availability, or
any other relevant details. By
promptly addressing their
queries, you help them make

informed decisions, and this transparency can foster trust and increase the likelihood of a successful transaction.

☐ Stand out from competitors: In a competitive marketplace, a prompt response can differentiate you from other sellers. Buyers appreciate sellers who are responsive and attentive to their needs. By demonstrating your professionalism and willingness to provide assistance, you increase the chances of capturing their attention and winning their business.

To ensure prompt responses, consider the following strategies:

☐ Enable notifications: Enable notifications on your device or browser to receive immediate alerts when you receive inquiries or messages on Facebook Marketplace. This allows you to respond promptly, even when you're not actively browsing the platform.

☐ Set dedicated response times: Establish specific time slots throughout the day to respond to inquiries and messages. This helps you manage your time effectively and ensures that you consistently provide timely responses.

☐ Prepare template responses: For frequently asked questions or common inquiries, create template responses that can be personalized and used as a starting point for your replies. This helps streamline your responses and ensures consistency while still allowing for personalization.

- ☐ Be clear and concise: When responding, be clear, concise, and helpful in your communication. Address the buyer's question or concern directly, and provide the information they need in a straightforward manner. Avoid jargon or overly technical language that may confuse or overwhelm the buyer.

- ☐ Manage expectations: If you are unable to provide an immediate response due to unforeseen circumstances or if additional research is required, acknowledge the inquiry and let the buyer know when they can expect a detailed response. Managing expectations and keeping buyers informed can help prevent frustration and maintain a positive customer experience.

Remember, prompt responses not only apply to initial inquiries but also extend throughout the entire communication and transaction process. Be responsive during negotiations, confirmations, and any follow-up discussions to maintain a high level of customer service.

By prioritizing prompt responses to inquiries and messages on Facebook Marketplace, you demonstrate professionalism, build trust, and increase the chances of successful transactions. Your timely and helpful interactions can make a significant impact on potential buyers and set you apart from the competition.

2. Clear and Detailed Descriptions: Craft compelling product descriptions that highlight key features, benefits, and any unique selling points. Use language that resonates with your target audience and provides the

information they need to make a purchasing decision.

Crafting clear and detailed descriptions is essential for effectively showcasing your products on Facebook Marketplace. A well-written description helps potential buyers understand the key features, benefits, and unique selling points of your product, making it easier for them to make an informed purchasing decision. Here are some tips to create compelling and informative product descriptions:

- Identify your target audience: Understand who your target audience is and tailor your description to their preferences and needs. Consider their demographics, interests, and motivations. Use language and tone that resonates with them, ensuring your description speaks directly to their interests and addresses their pain points.

- ☐ Highlight key features and benefits: Clearly outline the key features of your product and emphasize the benefits that customers will gain from using it. Explain how your product solves a problem, improves their lives, or fulfills a specific need. Focus on the unique aspects that differentiate your product from competitors and make it valuable to potential buyers.

- ☐ Use descriptive language: Paint a vivid picture with your words to help potential buyers visualize the product. Use descriptive adjectives and adverbs to convey the product's attributes, such as its appearance, size, color, texture, or performance. For example, instead of saying "a comfortable chair," you could say "a plush, ergonomic chair with padded armrests for ultimate comfort."

☐ Provide accurate specifications: Include relevant technical details, dimensions, materials, and any other specifications that potential buyers may find important. This information helps them assess whether the product meets their specific requirements and ensures transparency in your listing.

☐ Incorporate storytelling: Engage potential buyers by sharing the story behind your product. Explain its origin, inspiration, or the problem it aims to solve. Storytelling adds a personal touch and creates an emotional connection with buyers, making your product more memorable and compelling.

- Anticipate and answer potential questions: Think about the questions potential buyers may have and address them preemptively in your description. This can include information about shipping, return policies, warranties, or any other details that might impact their decision-making process. Anticipating and answering these questions upfront can help build trust and minimize uncertainties.
- Format for readability: Use bullet points, subheadings, and paragraphs to organize your description and make it easy to skim. Break down information into digestible chunks to enhance readability. A well-structured description allows potential buyers to quickly find the information they need and

encourages them to read the entire description.

☐ Use keywords strategically: Incorporate relevant keywords in your description to improve discoverability in search results. Think about the terms potential buyers would use when searching for products like yours and naturally integrate them into your description. However, avoid overstuffing keywords as it can make the description sound unnatural and affect readability.

☐ Include high-quality images: Supplement your description with high-quality images that showcase the product from different angles, highlighting its features and details. Images provide visual reinforcement and help potential buyers visualize the product, contributing to a more engaging and informative listing.

☐ Proofread and edit: Before publishing your description, proofread it carefully to correct any spelling or grammatical errors. Ensure that the information is accurate and up to date. A polished, error-free description demonstrates professionalism and attention to detail.

Regularly review and update your product descriptions to ensure they remain accurate and compelling. As market trends or customer preferences change, it's important to adapt your descriptions to stay relevant and competitive.

By crafting clear, detailed, and compelling product descriptions on Facebook Marketplace, you increase the chances of capturing the attention of potential buyers, engaging them with your product's unique value proposition, and ultimately driving successful transactions.

3. Professionalism and Politeness: Maintain a professional and friendly tone when communicating with potential buyers. Be courteous, address their queries, and provide additional information if requested.

   Maintaining professionalism and politeness in your interactions with potential buyers on Facebook Marketplace is essential for establishing a positive impression and fostering trust. A courteous and friendly tone not only reflects your commitment to excellent customer service but also creates a more pleasant buying experience. Here are some guidelines to ensure professionalism and politeness in your communication:

- [ ] Use proper greetings and salutations: Begin your communication with a polite greeting, such as "Hello" or "Hi," followed by the buyer's name if available. Using a friendly and respectful tone from the start sets a positive tone for the conversation.
- [ ] Respond promptly: Aim to respond to inquiries and messages in a timely manner. Even if you cannot provide an immediate answer, acknowledge the buyer's message promptly and let them know when they can expect a more detailed response. This shows that you value their time and are attentive to their needs.
- [ ] Be courteous and respectful: Always maintain a polite and respectful tone in your messages. Use courteous phrases like "Please," "Thank

you," and "You're welcome" to convey your appreciation and consideration. Even if the buyer has specific demands or requests, respond in a respectful manner and address their concerns professionally.

☐ Address queries and provide additional information: Take the time to thoroughly understand and address the buyer's queries or concerns. Provide accurate and detailed information to help them make an informed decision. If requested, be proactive in sharing additional details, such as product specifications, shipping options, or return policies. Clear and comprehensive answers demonstrate your commitment to transparency and customer satisfaction.

- Avoid jargon and use clear language: Ensure that your communication is easily understood by using clear and concise language. Avoid industry-specific jargon or technical terms that may confuse the buyer. Use simple, everyday language that conveys your message effectively.
- Be patient and understanding: Some buyers may have specific requirements or concerns. Practice patience and understanding when addressing their needs. If a buyer has multiple questions or requires additional assistance, take the time to answer each inquiry thoroughly. Your willingness to provide support can leave a lasting positive impression.
- Handle disagreements or issues calmly: In the event of a disagreement or issue, remain

calm and professional in your communication. Address concerns or complaints promptly and work toward finding a resolution. Taking a proactive and customer-centric approach can help diffuse tensions and maintain a positive buying experience.

- [ ] Use proper grammar and spelling: Pay attention to your grammar, punctuation, and spelling when communicating with potential buyers. Proper grammar and spelling enhance readability and convey professionalism. Proofread your messages before sending them to ensure they are error-free.

- [ ] Sign off with a polite closing: Conclude your communication with a courteous closing, such as "Best regards," "Sincerely," or "Thank you." This adds a personal touch and leaves a positive final impression.

Remember, every interaction on Facebook Marketplace contributes to your online reputation as a seller. Professionalism and politeness not only help you attract and retain customers but also promote positive word-of-mouth recommendations and repeat business.

By maintaining a professional and friendly tone in your communication, you establish yourself as a reliable and trustworthy seller. This fosters a positive buying experience, encourages potential buyers to feel confident in their decision to transact with you, and ultimately increases the chances of successful transactions on Facebook Marketplace.

4. Accurate Availability and Pricing:
   Ensure that your listing's availability
   and pricing information is up to date.
   If an item is no longer available,
   remove the listing promptly to avoid
   disappointing potential buyers.

   Maintaining accurate
   availability and pricing information in
   your listings on Facebook
   Marketplace is crucial for establishing
   trust and preventing frustration among
   potential buyers. By promptly
   updating your listings and removing
   items that are no longer available, you
   demonstrate transparency and respect
   for the buyer's time. Here are some
   important considerations:

   ☐ Regularly review your
     inventory: Keep a close eye on
     your inventory and review it
     regularly to ensure that the
     items you have listed on
     Facebook Marketplace are still
     available for sale. If an item has

been sold or is no longer in stock, take immediate action to update your listing accordingly.

☐ Remove sold items promptly: When an item is sold, remove the listing as soon as possible to avoid misleading potential buyers. Leaving sold items listed can lead to frustration and negative experiences for buyers who may reach out or express interest in a product that is no longer available. By promptly removing sold items, you demonstrate professionalism and consideration for the buyer's needs.

☐ Update availability status: If you have multiple quantities of an item, clearly indicate the available quantity in your listing. Regularly update the availability status to reflect accurate stock levels. If an item is temporarily out of stock but

will be replenished soon,
consider mentioning this in the
listing to manage buyer
expectations.

☐ Price accuracy and adjustments:
Ensure that the pricing
information in your listings is
accurate and up to date. If you
need to adjust the price of an
item, make sure to do so
promptly. If there are any
promotions, discounts, or
special offers applicable to
specific items, clearly mention
them in the listing. Accurate
pricing information helps
potential buyers make informed
decisions and avoids any
confusion or dissatisfaction
later on.

☐ Be transparent about shipping
or pickup options: If you offer
shipping or local pickup
options, clearly outline the
details and any associated costs

in your listing. Ensure that the information provided is accurate and aligns with your current policies. If there are any changes to shipping methods or costs, promptly update your listing to reflect the latest information.

☐ Regularly review and update your listings: Take the time to review your listings periodically to ensure all the information is accurate and up to date. This includes availability, pricing, shipping information, and any other relevant details. Regularly updating your listings demonstrates your commitment to providing a reliable and trustworthy buying experience.

☐ Communicate changes to interested buyers: If a potential buyer has already expressed interest in an item that becomes unavailable, notify them promptly and apologize for the inconvenience. Offer alternatives or provide information on when the item might become available again, if applicable. This proactive communication can help manage expectations and maintain positive relationships with potential buyers.

By maintaining accurate availability and pricing information, you create a transparent and trustworthy shopping experience on Facebook Marketplace. This increases the likelihood of successful transactions and positive feedback from satisfied buyers. Additionally, accurate listings contribute to building a strong reputation as a reliable seller, encouraging repeat business and attracting new customers.

Remember, keeping your listings up to date requires ongoing attention and diligence. Regularly reviewing and updating your inventory and promptly removing sold items will help you provide an optimal buying experience for potential customers on Facebook Marketplace.

IMPORTANCE OF EFFECTIVE COMMUNICATION

Effective communication plays a vital role in enhancing sales and customer satisfaction on Facebook Marketplace. Here's an exploration of the benefits and strategies for improving communication to boost your success:

Improving Customer Satisfaction: Clear and responsive communication contributes to improved customer satisfaction in the following ways:

1. **Creates Trust:** Prompt and transparent communication builds trust with potential buyers. When they receive timely and accurate information, they feel more confident in making a purchase.

2. **Provides Effective Solutions:** Effective communication allows you to understand customer needs, address their concerns, and provide appropriate solutions. This leads to higher customer satisfaction and positive reviews.

3. **Encourages Engagement:** Engaging with potential buyers in a friendly and helpful manner fosters a positive customer experience. By actively responding to inquiries and being accessible, you encourage further engagement and increase the likelihood of successful transactions.

Managing Communication: To effectively manage communication on Facebook Marketplace, consider the following strategies:

1. **Set Goals:** Clearly define your communication goals, such as response time, tone, and level of detail, to ensure consistency and professionalism in your interactions.

2. **Utilize Subscriptions:** Subscribe to notifications and alerts to stay informed about new messages, inquiries, and comments on your listings. This allows for timely responses and minimizes missed opportunities.

3. **Participate in Councils/Forums:** Join relevant groups, forums, or councils related to your product niche. Actively participate in discussions, answer questions, and share your expertise to establish yourself as a trusted authority and build credibility.

Effective Communication Skills for Online Selling: Developing effective communication skills specific to online selling can significantly impact your success. Consider the following skills:

- Pay full attention to the buyer's needs and inquiries.

- Practice active listening by demonstrating understanding and asking relevant follow-up questions.

- Interpret and respond to non-verbal cues, both from the buyer and in your own communication.

- Master the nuance of voice tones to convey enthusiasm, empathy, and professionalism.

- Show empathy and understanding toward customers' concerns and needs.

- Understand the unspoken context and underlying messages in communication.

- Provide specific and detailed information to address buyer inquiries.

- Establish yourself as a subject matter expert by showcasing your knowledge and expertise.

- Show genuine curiosity and interest in understanding customers' requirements.

- Avoid assuming that you know everything; be open to learning and adapting.

- Assume good intent and maintain a positive and helpful attitude.

- Always be honest and transparent in your communication.

- Avoid making assumptions and seek clarification when needed.

- Be persistent in following up with potential buyers, but avoid being pushy or pestering.

- Be comfortable with moments of silence, allowing buyers to process information and make decisions.

USING FACEBOOK ADS FOR PROMOTING LISTINGS

Facebook Ads provide a powerful advertising platform to promote your listings and reach a wider audience on Facebook Marketplace. Here's a breakdown of how to use Facebook's advertising platform effectively:

What are Facebook Ads in the Marketplace? Facebook Ads in the Marketplace are paid advertisements that allow you to promote your listings to a targeted audience. These ads appear within the Marketplace feed, increasing the visibility of your products and reaching potential buyers who are actively browsing the Marketplace.

Benefits of Ads in Marketplace: Using Facebook Ads in the Marketplace offers several benefits for sellers:

☐ Free Listings vs. Promoted Listings: While standard listings on Facebook Marketplace are free, promoting your listings through ads provides a significant advantage. By investing in ads, you can boost the visibility of your listings and increase the chances of potential buyers discovering your products. This enhanced exposure can lead to higher engagement and more sales opportunities.

☐ Reach Your Customers Where They Actively Shop: Facebook Marketplace has a vast user base consisting of individuals actively searching for products. By utilizing ads, you can target these users and showcase your listings to a highly relevant audience. This targeted approach ensures that your ads are seen by potential buyers who are already in a shopping mindset, improving the likelihood of conversions.

☐ Easily Scale Ads with Automatic Placements: Facebook's ad platform allows you to automate the placement of your ads across various locations within Facebook and its partner networks. This means that your listings can be shown in the most effective locations where your target audience is likely to engage with them. By leveraging automatic placements, you can save time and effort while ensuring maximum reach for your ads.

☐ Get More Efficient Outcomes: Facebook offers robust targeting capabilities that enable you to reach the right audience for your products. With options to define your target audience based on demographics, interests, behaviors, and more, you can narrow down your ad reach to individuals who are most likely to be interested in what you offer. This precision targeting helps you achieve more efficient outcomes by focusing your ad spend on the most relevant audience segments, increasing the chances of conversions and maximizing your return on investment.

☐ Track and Optimize Performance: Facebook's ad platform provides comprehensive analytics and reporting tools that allow you to track the performance of your Marketplace ads. You can monitor key metrics such as impressions, clicks, conversions, and cost per result. This data-driven approach empowers you to analyze the effectiveness of your ad campaigns, identify areas for improvement, and make data-backed decisions to optimize your ads for better results.

By leveraging Facebook Ads in the Marketplace, sellers can take advantage of the platform's extensive reach, powerful targeting capabilities, and robust ad management tools. These benefits enable sellers to effectively promote their listings, connect with a relevant audience, and drive more conversions, ultimately enhancing their success on the Facebook Marketplace platform.

Steps to Using Facebook Ads: To use Facebook Ads to promote your listings, follow these general steps:

1. **Create a Facebook Business Page:** If you don't have one already, create a Facebook Business Page that represents your brand or store.

2. **Access Ads Manager:** Go to Facebook Ads Manager, which is a platform for managing and creating ads on Facebook.

3. **Choose Your Objective:** Select the objective that aligns with your goals, such as increasing brand awareness, driving website traffic, or generating conversions.

4. **Define Your Target Audience:** Set specific targeting parameters to reach your ideal customers, including demographics, interests, and behaviors.

5. **Set Your Budget and Schedule:** Determine your ad budget and choose the duration and schedule for running your ads.

6. **Create Compelling Ad Content:** Design engaging ad creative that showcases your products, includes clear and enticing descriptions, and uses high-quality visuals.

7. **Choose Automatic Placements:** Select automatic ad placements to let Facebook optimize the delivery of your ads across various placements, including Facebook, Instagram, and Audience Network.

8. **Monitor and Optimize:** Continuously monitor the performance of your ads and make

necessary adjustments to optimize their effectiveness.

Best Practices: Here are some best practices to consider when using Facebook Ads in the Marketplace:

- **High-Quality Visuals:** Use high-resolution images or videos that showcase your products and grab attention.

- **Compelling Ad Copy:** Craft compelling ad descriptions that highlight the unique features, benefits, and value of your products.

- **Target Audience:** Define your target audience carefully based on demographics, interests, and behaviors to ensure your ads reach the right people.

- **Testing and Optimization:** Test different ad variations, targeting options, and messaging to identify what resonates best with your audience and optimize your ad performance.

- **Consistent Branding:** Maintain consistent branding across your ads, landing pages, and listings to establish brand recognition and trust.

-

IMPORTANT METRICS TO TRACK

When running Facebook Ads to promote your Marketplace listings, it's crucial to track and analyze important metrics to assess the effectiveness of your campaigns and make data-driven decisions. Here are some key metrics to track:

1. **Frequency:** Frequency measures the average number of times your ad is shown to each person in your target audience. It helps you understand how often your ad is being seen and if it

might be reaching a point of ad fatigue.

2. **Cost per Click (CPC):** CPC indicates the cost you pay for each click on your ad. It helps evaluate the efficiency of your ad spend and compare the cost-effectiveness of different campaigns or ad sets.

3. **Click-Through Rate (CTR):** CTR measures the percentage of people who click on your ad after seeing it. A high CTR indicates that your ad is compelling and resonating with your target audience.

4. **Conversion Rate:** Conversion rate measures the percentage of people who take the desired action, such as making a purchase or submitting a form, after clicking on your ad. It reflects the effectiveness of your ad in driving desired outcomes.

5. **Return on Ad Spend (ROAS):** ROAS calculates the revenue

generated for every dollar spent on advertising. It helps you determine the profitability of your ad campaigns and compare their performance.

6. **Cost per Acquisition (CPA):** CPA measures the average cost of acquiring a customer or achieving a specific conversion goal. It enables you to evaluate the cost-effectiveness of your campaigns in acquiring new customers or achieving desired outcomes.

7. **Engagement Metrics:** Metrics such as likes, comments, shares, and video views indicate how well your ad content resonates with your audience and encourages engagement.

8. **Audience Demographics:** Analyzing demographic data, such as age, gender, location, and interests, can provide insights into which segments of your target audience are responding most positively to your ads.

9. **Ad Placement Performance:** Assess how your ads perform across different placements (e.g., Facebook News Feed, Instagram, Audience Network) to optimize your budget allocation and improve ad performance.

10. **Attribution Metrics:** Consider tracking metrics like view-through conversions and assisted conversions to understand the impact of your ads at various touchpoints in the customer journey.

Remember, it's important to select the metrics that align with your specific goals and objectives. Regularly monitor and analyze these metrics to identify trends, make data-driven optimizations, and maximize the effectiveness of your Facebook Ads campaigns.

Hey Marketplace Explorer!

Congratulations on delving into this amazing book. I hope you're finding it as thrilling and enlightening as your journey through the dynamic world of selling on the Facebook Marketplace.

As you navigate through the treasure trove of tips, tricks, and insider insights, I'd love to take a moment to invite you to share your thoughts with fellow Facebook marketers. Your feedback is like a guiding light for others embarking on this same adventure.

Why Your Review Matters:

1. **Help Future Marketers:** Your experience could be the compass someone else needs to navigate the Facebook Marketplace terrain successfully.

2. **Fuel for Jeff's Next Expedition:** Jeff thrives on your insights! Let him know how his guide has influenced your approach to online selling.

3. **Build a Community of Sellers:** Join the ranks of fellow sellers sharing their experiences, creating a

community that thrives on shared knowledge.

Simply Share Your Marketplace Review By Scanning the QR Code With Your Phone Camera Here:

SEO FOR YOUR LISTINGS: KEYWORDS AND DESCRIPTION

To optimize your listings for search and improve their visibility on Facebook Marketplace, it's important to use relevant keywords strategically. Here are some tips on how to optimize your listings using keywords and descriptions:

1. **Know Your Buyer:** Understand your target audience and the specific keywords they might use when searching for products similar to yours. Put yourself in their shoes and think about the words or phrases they would likely use in their search.

2. **Keyword Research:** Conduct keyword research to identify relevant and high-traffic keywords related to your products. Use tools like Facebook Marketplace search, Google

Trends, or keyword research tools to discover popular and trending keywords.

3. **Using Keywords in Your FB Marketplace Listing:** Incorporate your target keywords naturally into the title and description of your listing. Ensure that the keywords accurately represent your product and provide a clear description of its features, benefits, and condition.

4. **Write a Compelling Description:** Along with keywords, craft a compelling and detailed description that highlights the unique selling points of your product. Use persuasive language to attract potential buyers and provide all the necessary information they might need to make a purchasing decision.

5. **Use Additional Sales Strategies:** While SEO is important, there are other strategies you can employ to

increase sales on Facebook
Marketplace. These include:

- Captivating Product Photos:
  Use high-quality, well-lit
  images that showcase your
  product from different angles
  and highlight its key features.

- Competitive Pricing: Set your
  prices competitively based on
  market research and the value
  of your product. Consider
  offering discounts or
  promotions to attract more
  buyers.

- Prompt and Professional
  Communication: Respond to
  inquiries and messages from
  potential buyers in a timely and
  courteous manner. Clear any
  doubts they may have and
  provide excellent customer
  service.

- Positive Reviews and Social Proof: Encourage satisfied customers to leave reviews or testimonials on your Marketplace profile. Positive reviews can build trust and credibility for your products.

- Share Listings on social media: Promote your listings on your social media channels to reach a wider audience and attract potential buyers who may not be actively searching on Facebook Marketplace.

Remember, optimizing your listings for search is just one aspect of increasing sales on Facebook Marketplace. It's essential to employ a holistic approach by combining SEO techniques with other effective sales strategies.

HOW TO USE SOCIAL PROOF TO BOOST SALES

To boost sales on Facebook Marketplace, leveraging social proof can be highly effective in building trust and credibility among potential buyers. Here's how you can utilize social proof to enhance your sales:

1. **What is Social Proof?** Social proof refers to the influence and validation that individuals derive from the actions and opinions of others. It serves as evidence that a product or service is trustworthy and reliable.

2. **Why is Social Proof Important?** Social proof plays a crucial role in building trust with potential buyers. When people see positive feedback or endorsements from others, it instills confidence in the quality and value of your products, making them more likely to make a purchase.

3. **Customer Reviews:** Encourage satisfied customers to leave reviews and ratings on your Facebook Marketplace listings. Positive reviews provide social proof and act as testimonials that can influence the purchasing decisions of other potential buyers.

4. **User-Generated Content:** Share user-generated content, such as photos or videos of customers using or showcasing your products. This type of content demonstrates real-life experiences and can create a sense of authenticity and trust.

5. **Influencer Endorsements:** Collaborate with influencers or industry experts who have a relevant audience. Their endorsement of your products can significantly impact the purchasing decisions of their followers.

6. **Industry Awards:** Highlight any industry awards or recognition your business has received. Awards serve as external validation and can boost your credibility and reputation.

7. **Business Accomplishments and Recognition:** Showcase any notable achievements or milestones your business has accomplished, such as partnerships with reputable brands or media features. This kind of recognition can enhance your brand's reputation and build trust with potential buyers.

Remember to showcase social proof consistently across your Facebook Marketplace listings and engage with customers who provide feedback or reviews. Responding to reviews, whether positive or negative, shows that you value customer input and are committed to providing excellent service.

KEEPING YOUR LISTINGS ACTIVE

Regularly updating and keeping your listings active is crucial for maximizing your success on platforms like Facebook Marketplace. By maintaining an active presence, you increase visibility, engage potential buyers, and demonstrate your commitment to providing up-to-date and relevant offerings. Here's why it's important and how you can achieve it:

1. Maintaining Relevance: Online marketplaces are dynamic environments where trends, preferences, and competition can change rapidly. By updating your listings, you can ensure that your products or services remain relevant to the needs and interests of potential buyers. Regular updates allow you to showcase new inventory, highlight

promotions, and adjust pricing to stay competitive.

2. Visibility and Discoverability: Active listings tend to receive better visibility in search results and browsing categories. Platforms often prioritize recent and updated listings to provide users with fresh content. By consistently refreshing your listings, you increase the chances of attracting potential buyers who are actively searching for products or services like yours.

3. Trust and Credibility: When buyers see that your listings are regularly updated, they gain confidence in your business. It demonstrates your commitment and professionalism, creating a positive impression that can lead to higher trust levels and increased sales. Conversely, outdated listings may raise doubts about the reliability of your offerings.

4. Adapting to Market Changes: The market landscape is dynamic, and consumer preferences can evolve over time. By keeping your listings active and updated, you can respond to these changes promptly. You can modify product descriptions, images, and pricing to align with market demands, ensuring that your offerings remain attractive and competitive.

To achieve active listings, consider the following tips:

a. Regularly Review and Update: Set aside dedicated time to review your listings and make necessary updates. Ensure that product descriptions, images, and pricing reflect the current state of your offerings. Remove any outdated information or discontinued products.

b. Optimize Listing Titles and Descriptions: Use relevant keywords in your titles and descriptions to improve search visibility.

Research popular search terms within your niche and incorporate them strategically. This can help potential buyers find your listings more easily.

c. Refresh Images: Visual appeal is crucial in online marketplaces. Regularly update product images to showcase your offerings in the best possible light. High-quality and visually appealing images can grab attention and entice buyers to explore your listings further.

d. Monitor and Respond to Customer Inquiries: Actively engage with potential buyers by promptly responding to inquiries and messages. By providing timely and helpful responses, you create a positive impression and increase the likelihood of converting inquiries into sales.

e. Utilize Promotional Tools: Take advantage of promotional tools offered by the platform, such as discounts, featured listings, or sponsored placements. These options can help boost visibility and attract more potential buyers to your listings.

By implementing these strategies, you can ensure that your listings remain active, relevant, and appealing to potential buyers. Regular updates demonstrate your commitment to providing the best possible offerings and improve your chances of success on platforms like Facebook Marketplace.

Summary: Marketing Techniques to Enhance Sales

In the above chapter, we delved into various marketing strategies to enhance your sales on Facebook Marketplace. We discussed the importance of effective communication in building trust and customer satisfaction. We explored how to leverage Facebook ads to promote your listings, reach your target audience, and track important metrics for campaign success. Additionally, we explored the significance of SEO for optimizing your listings, using relevant keywords, and increasing your visibility in search results. We also emphasized the power of social proof in building trust and credibility, leveraging customer reviews, user-generated content, and industry recognition. Lastly, we highlighted the importance of regularly updating and keeping your listings active to maintain relevance, visibility, and customer engagement.

Key Takeaways:

1. Effective communication plays a vital role in building trust, resolving issues, and encouraging customer engagement.

2. Facebook ads provide an effective way to promote your listings and reach your target audience, with various benefits and best practices to consider.

3. Optimizing your listings with relevant keywords and descriptions can

improve your search visibility and attract potential buyers.

4. Social proof, including customer reviews, endorsements, and business achievements, can significantly enhance trust and boost sales.

5. Regularly updating and keeping your listings active is crucial for maintaining relevance, visibility, and customer engagement.

In the next chapter, we will focus on the most commonly sold items on the platform.

CHAPTER FIVE

THE MOST COMMONLY SOLD ITEMS AND WHY THEY SELL

Chapter Hook: Let's dive into the fascinating world of Facebook Marketplace and explore the most commonly sold items on the platform. From the weird and bizarre to the practical and in-demand, Facebook Marketplace is a treasure trove of unique products that cater to a wide range of interests and needs. Get ready to uncover the peculiar, popular, and profitable items that have captured the attention of buyers on Facebook Marketplace.

THE PSYCHOLOGY BEHIND SELLING ON FACEBOOK MARKETPLACE

Understanding the factors that influence buyer behavior on Facebook Marketplace is essential for sellers looking to maximize their success on the platform. By grasping the psychological principles that drive purchasing decisions, sellers can tailor their strategies to meet customer needs effectively. Let's explore the psychology behind selling on Facebook Marketplace and the key factors that shape buyer behavior.

1. Case Study: Factors Influencing the Consumer's Intention of Buying through Facebook - A Study on Dhaka City. Referencing the case study on factors influencing consumer buying behavior on Facebook in Dhaka City provides valuable insights into the specific dynamics of this platform. Analyzing the study's

findings can shed light on the motivations, preferences, and decision-making processes of Facebook Marketplace users in that particular context.

2. Overview of Factors Influencing Buyer Behavior. There are several common factors that influence buyer behavior on Facebook Marketplace. These factors include:

☐ Social Proof: Buyers are influenced by the opinions, reviews, and recommendations of others. Positive social proof, such as customer reviews and ratings, can significantly impact buyer decisions and build trust in a seller's offerings.

☐ Price and Value Perception: Buyers consider the price of a product or service and weigh it against the perceived value they will receive. Sellers who can effectively communicate the value and benefits of their offerings are more likely to attract buyers.

☐ Convenience and Accessibility: Buyers are drawn to listings that offer convenience and easy accessibility. This can include factors such as clear product descriptions, high-quality images, and responsive communication from the seller.

☐ Trust and Reputation: Building trust is crucial for successful selling on Facebook Marketplace. Buyers seek sellers with a positive reputation, reliable customer service, and transparent business practices.

☐ Emotional Appeal: Emotional factors play a significant role in buyer behavior. Buyers may be motivated by their desires, aspirations, and emotional connection to a product. Sellers who tap into these emotions can create a stronger appeal for their offerings.

By incorporating these psychological insights into your selling strategies on Facebook Marketplace, you can align your approach with the motivations and preferences of potential buyers. Understanding the factors that influence buyer behavior empowers sellers to optimize their listings, establish trust, and create compelling offers that resonate with their target audience.

ANALYZING TOP-SELLING ITEMS AND WHY THEY'RE POPULAR

To understand the characteristics of top-selling items on Facebook Marketplace and why they sell well, let's explore a range of popular categories and the reasons behind their success.

1. Furniture: Furniture items are in high demand on Facebook Marketplace

due to their practicality and cost-effectiveness. Many buyers look for affordable second-hand furniture options, allowing them to furnish their homes without breaking the bank.

2. Clothing, Shoes, Accessories: Fashion items, including clothing, shoes, and accessories, are popular due to the wide variety of styles available and the potential for finding unique and affordable pieces. Buyers often seek fashionable items at lower prices compared to traditional retail stores.

3. Books: Books continue to be sought-after items on Facebook Marketplace. Buyers appreciate the convenience and cost savings of purchasing used books, and the platform provides an opportunity to discover rare or out-of-print editions.

4. Seasonal Products: Seasonal products, such as holiday decorations or outdoor equipment, experience high

demand during specific times of the year. Buyers look for deals on items that are in season, allowing them to save money and prepare for upcoming events.

5. Home Goods: Home goods, including kitchenware, decor, and appliances, are popular on Facebook Marketplace. Buyers can find affordable options to furnish and decorate their homes while enjoying the convenience of local pickup.

6. Sports and Fitness Equipment: With the growing interest in health and fitness, sports and fitness equipment sell well on Facebook Marketplace. Buyers can find discounted items, such as exercise machines or sporting gear, to support their active lifestyles.

7. Trading Cards: Collectible trading cards, including sports cards or trading card games, have a dedicated market on Facebook Marketplace.

Buyers are often enthusiasts looking to complete their collections or find rare cards.

8. Tools: Tools are essential items for DIY enthusiasts and professionals alike. Buyers on Facebook Marketplace often search for used tools at lower prices compared to buying new ones, allowing them to save money while still acquiring high-quality equipment.

9. Toys: Parents and collectors frequently browse Facebook Marketplace for affordable toys. Second-hand toys in good condition offer a budget-friendly option for parents, while collectors may find unique or vintage items.

10. Baby Supplies: Baby supplies, including strollers, cribs, and clothing, are in high demand on Facebook Marketplace. New parents often seek cost-effective options for baby

essentials, and the platform provides a convenient marketplace to find such items.

11. Jewelry: Jewelry, both costume and fine, can attract buyers looking for unique pieces or special gifts. Facebook Marketplace offers a platform for sellers to showcase their jewelry collections and reach potential buyers.

12. Electronics: Electronics, such as smartphones, laptops, and gaming consoles, remain popular on Facebook Marketplace. Buyers often seek affordable pre-owned devices or accessories, and sellers can capitalize on this demand.

13. Vehicles: While selling vehicles requires additional considerations, Facebook Marketplace serves as a platform for connecting buyers and sellers. The convenience of local listings and the potential for finding

good deals make it a popular category.

14. Instruments: Musical instruments, such as guitars, keyboards, and drums, have a dedicated market on Facebook Marketplace. Buyers, including musicians and aspiring artists, can find affordable instruments to pursue their passions.

15. More Best-Selling Items: For a comprehensive list of best-selling items on Facebook Marketplace and further insights into their popularity, you can explore the provided resources. These sources offer valuable information on popular categories and the reasons behind their success.

By understanding the characteristics and reasons why these items sell well, sellers can focus their efforts on offering products within these categories or catering to similar buyer preferences. Adapting to consumer demands and aligning product offerings with popular categories can enhance sales and maximize success on Facebook Marketplace.

LEVERAGING TRENDS FOR YOUR SUCCESS

Keeping up with trends is crucial for success in the Facebook Marketplace. In a dynamic and ever-changing marketplace, trends have a significant impact on buyer behavior, demand for specific products, and ultimately, sales. Let's explore why staying current with trends is important and how it can benefit your business on Facebook Marketplace.

1. Understanding Buyer Behavior: Trends influence buyer behavior by shaping their preferences, needs, and expectations. By staying updated on trends, you gain insights into what

buyers are seeking and can align your product offerings accordingly. This understanding allows you to cater to their desires and stay ahead of the competition.

2. Capitalizing on Demand: Trends create shifts in demand for certain products or categories. By identifying emerging trends, you can capitalize on the increased demand and adjust your inventory or marketing strategies accordingly. This proactive approach enables you to offer in-demand products, resulting in higher sales and customer satisfaction.

3. Standing Out from Competitors: In a competitive marketplace, staying current with trends helps your business stand out from competitors. By incorporating trending elements into your listings, such as popular styles, keywords, or themes, you can attract more attention and engage with potential buyers effectively. This

differentiation sets you apart and positions your business as relevant and up-to-date.

4. Anticipating Future Opportunities: Trends often provide insights into upcoming opportunities and market gaps. By keeping a pulse on industry trends, you can identify emerging niches, product innovations, or consumer needs that are not yet fully addressed. This foresight allows you to position your business to meet future demands and be ahead of the curve.

5. Enhancing Customer Engagement: Staying current with trends enables you to connect with your target audience on a deeper level. By understanding their interests and preferences, you can create relevant and engaging content, promotions, and experiences. This customer-centric approach fosters stronger

relationships, increases trust, and drives repeat business.

By leveraging trends, you can tap into the evolving marketplace dynamics and align your business strategy with changing consumer preferences. Staying updated on trends not only allows you to meet customer demands effectively but also positions your business as a trendsetter and industry leader.

Staying Informed: How to Keep Up with Current Trends

To stay ahead of the curve and leverage the latest trends on Facebook Marketplace, it's essential to stay informed and up-to-date. Here are various ways you can stay informed about the latest trends:

1. Follow Relevant News Sources: Keep an eye on industry-specific news sources, blogs, and publications that cover topics related to your niche.

These sources often provide insights into emerging trends, consumer preferences, and market dynamics. Set up alerts or subscribe to newsletters to receive regular updates directly in your inbox.

2. Join Industry Groups on Social Media: Participate in industry-specific groups and communities on social media platforms like Facebook and LinkedIn. These groups offer a wealth of information and discussions related to your industry. Engage with other members, share experiences, and stay updated on the latest trends, news, and best practices.

3. Track Top Sellers on the Marketplace: Monitor the listings and activities of top sellers on Facebook Marketplace within your industry. Pay attention to their product offerings, pricing strategies, and promotional tactics. By observing successful sellers, you can gain insights into trending products,

popular categories, and effective
selling techniques.

4. Utilize Facebook's Insights and
Analytics Tools: Leverage the
analytics tools provided by Facebook
to gain valuable data about your
listings and target audience. Facebook
Insights provides metrics on
engagement, reach, and
demographics, helping you
understand which products or content
resonate with your audience.
Analyzing these insights can reveal
trends and patterns that can inform
your marketing and product strategies.

5. Attend Trade Shows and Industry
Events: Participate in trade shows,
exhibitions, conferences, and
seminars relevant to your industry.
These events provide opportunities to
network with industry experts,
discover new products and
technologies, and gain insights into
emerging trends. Stay updated on

upcoming events through industry associations or event directories.

6. Engage with Customers and Seek Feedback: Interacting with your customers directly can provide valuable insights into their preferences, needs, and feedback on your products. Engage with your audience through comments, messages, and reviews on Facebook Marketplace. Encourage feedback and suggestions to understand their evolving requirements and identify potential trends.

7. Monitor Social Media Trending Topics: Keep an eye on trending topics and hashtags on social media platforms, including Facebook, Instagram, Twitter, and TikTok. These trends often reflect consumer interests and can inspire ideas for product offerings or marketing campaigns. Stay active on social media and engage with trending

content to stay relevant and
connected.

Identifying Relevant Trends and Distinguishing Short-Term Fads from Long-Term Trends

Not all trends will be relevant to every seller or product category. It's important to identify which trends align with your product offerings and target audience to make informed business decisions. Here are some strategies to help you identify relevant trends and distinguish between short-term fads and long-term trends:

1. Understand Your Target Audience: Start by gaining a deep understanding of your target audience. Analyze their demographics, preferences, behavior, and purchasing patterns. This information will help you identify trends that are most likely to resonate

with your audience and impact their buying decisions.

2. Conduct Market Research: Engage in thorough market research to identify current and emerging trends in your industry. Explore industry reports, market studies, competitor analysis, and customer surveys to gather valuable insights. Look for patterns, shifts in consumer behavior, and emerging technologies or innovations that can influence your product category.

3. Monitor Consumer Behavior: Track consumer behavior and observe changes in their preferences and purchasing habits. Pay attention to shifts in demand, popular product categories, and emerging needs. Social listening tools and analytics platforms can provide real-time data and sentiment analysis, allowing you to identify emerging trends that align with your target audience.

4. Keep an Eye on Industry Influencers and Thought Leaders: Follow industry influencers, thought leaders, and experts in your niche. They often have their fingers on the pulse of the industry and can provide insights into emerging trends. Engage with their content, participate in discussions, and take note of their observations and predictions.

5. Stay Updated with Industry News and Publications: Regularly read industry-specific news, blogs, and publications to stay informed about the latest developments. These sources often highlight emerging trends, innovative products, and market dynamics. Subscribing to newsletters and setting up Google Alerts can ensure you receive timely updates.

6. Analyze Data and Metrics: Leverage data and metrics from your own business operations. Analyze sales data, customer feedback, website

analytics, and social media engagement to identify trends specific to your business. Look for patterns and correlations between certain products, marketing campaigns, or customer segments.

7. Look for Long-Term Patterns: Distinguishing between short-term fads and long-term trends requires a careful analysis of patterns over time. Look for trends that exhibit consistent growth and longevity, supported by reliable data and market research. Short-term fads often experience sudden spikes in popularity but quickly fade away, whereas long-term trends demonstrate sustainability and continued demand.

8. Evaluate External Factors: Consider external factors that can influence trends, such as technological advancements, economic conditions, cultural shifts, and regulatory changes. These factors can shape

consumer behavior and create opportunities for new trends to emerge or existing trends to evolve.

In this Chapter, we explored the topic of bestselling items on Facebook Marketplace and analyzed why they tend to sell well. We identified popular categories and discussed the factors that contribute to their success. By understanding the market demand and tailoring your listings accordingly, you can increase your chances of making successful sales on Facebook Marketplace.

Key Takeaways:

1. Identify popular categories: Certain categories consistently perform well on Facebook Marketplace. These include electronics, furniture, clothing and accessories, home appliances, and baby and children's items. By focusing on these categories, you can tap into existing demand and increase your chances of successful sales.

2. Quality and condition matter: Buyers on Facebook Marketplace seek good quality items in excellent condition. Ensure that your items are clean, functional, and accurately described in your listings. Providing detailed information and clear images helps build trust and attracts potential buyers.

3. Competitive pricing: Research the market and set competitive prices for your items. Pricing too high can deter buyers, while pricing too low might raise suspicions. Find the right balance by considering factors such as the item's condition, age, brand, and current market value.

4. Unique and niche offerings: Stand out from the competition by offering unique or niche items. These can attract buyers who are specifically seeking something different or hard to find. Consider specializing in a particular category or offering

customized or handmade products to cater to specific audiences.

5. Effective marketing techniques: Utilize effective marketing techniques to enhance the visibility and reach of your listings. This includes using high-quality images, crafting attention-grabbing titles, and utilizing keywords that potential buyers might search for. Promote your listings through social media and engage with interested buyers promptly.

In the next chapter, we will delve into managing Facebook Marketplace sales and negotiating with buyers. We will discuss strategies for effective communication, handling inquiries, and closing deals successfully. By mastering these skills, you can optimize your selling experience and increase your chances of achieving favorable outcomes. Get ready to enhance your sales management skills in the upcoming chapter!

CHAPTER SIX

MANAGING SALES AND NEGOTIATIONS

In this chapter, we will explore the art of managing sales and negotiations on Facebook Marketplace. Selling online can be a rewarding experience, but it also comes with its fair share of challenges. We will provide valuable insights and strategies to help you navigate through these challenges and ensure successful transactions.

HOW TO MANAGE YOUR SALES

When it comes to managing sales on Facebook Marketplace, utilizing a Customer Relationship Management (CRM) system can be a game-changer. A CRM system allows you to effectively manage interactions with your customers, keep track of orders, and maintain strong customer relationships. Here's how a CRM system can benefit your sales management efforts:

1. Organize and Analyze Customer Data: A CRM system enables you to centralize and organize customer data, including contact information, purchase history, and communication logs. This comprehensive view of your customers helps you understand their preferences and buying behavior, allowing you to tailor your approach and offer personalized recommendations.

2. Streamline Communication: With a CRM system, you can easily manage customer interactions in one place. It provides a unified inbox where you can track emails, messages, and other communication channels. This ensures that no details or customer inquiries slip through the cracks, leading to improved responsiveness and customer satisfaction.

3. Track Sales and Forecast Trends: CRM systems offer robust reporting and analytics capabilities. You can generate sales reports, track key performance indicators, and analyze trends in your sales data. This helps you identify patterns, forecast future sales, and make data-driven decisions to optimize your selling strategies on Facebook Marketplace.

4. Enhance Customer Service: A CRM system allows you to provide exceptional customer service. By having access to complete customer information, you can address their concerns promptly and efficiently. Additionally, you can set reminders and automate follow-ups, ensuring that you stay connected with your customers and nurture those relationships.

5. Improve Collaboration and Team Efficiency: If you have a team of sales professionals, a CRM system

facilitates collaboration and coordination. It enables team members to access and update customer data in real time, ensuring everyone is on the same page. This enhances efficiency, reduces duplication of efforts, and enables seamless handoffs between team members.

By leveraging a CRM system, you can effectively manage your sales processes, build stronger customer relationships, and ultimately drive success on Facebook Marketplace.

IMPLEMENT ORDER MANAGEMENT TOOLS

As your sales volume increases on Facebook Marketplace, it becomes important to have efficient order management processes in place. Implementing order management tools can greatly streamline your operations and ensure a seamless fulfillment experience. Here's why you should consider using order management software:

1. Centralize Order Tracking: Order management tools allow you to consolidate and track orders from multiple channels, including Facebook Marketplace. You can view all your incoming orders in one place, making it easier to manage and process them efficiently.

2. Inventory Management: Effective order management involves keeping track of your inventory levels. Order management software helps you monitor your stock levels, automatically updating them as orders are received and fulfilled. This ensures that you have accurate information about product availability and can avoid overselling or stockouts.

3. Streamline Shipping and Fulfillment: Order management tools often integrate with shipping carriers, enabling you to generate shipping labels, track shipments, and provide customers with order status updates. This streamlines the fulfillment process and enhances customer satisfaction by providing timely and accurate delivery information.

4. Order Customization and Personalization: Some order management tools offer customization options, allowing you to create personalized packing slips, invoices, and order confirmations. This adds a professional touch to your transactions and reinforces your brand identity.

5. Reporting and Analytics: Many order management software solutions provide reporting and analytics features. You can generate insights on sales performance, order trends, and

customer behavior. This data can help you make informed decisions, optimize your selling strategies, and identify opportunities for growth on Facebook Marketplace.

By implementing order management tools, you can effectively track and fulfill orders, streamline your shipping processes, and maintain better control over your inventory. This enables you to provide a smooth buying experience for your customers on Facebook Marketplace while maintaining operational efficiency.

MAINTAIN CLEAR COMMUNICATION

Maintaining clear and effective communication is essential when managing your sales on Facebook Marketplace. It helps build trust with your customers, fosters positive relationships, and ensures a smooth transaction process. Here are some strategies to maintain clear communication:

1. Be Transparent: Provide accurate and detailed information about your products, including prices, conditions, and any additional fees. Clearly communicate your return or refund policies, shipping options, and estimated delivery times. Transparency helps manage customer expectations and minimizes misunderstandings.

2. Promptly Respond to Inquiries: Respond to customer inquiries and messages in a timely manner. Aim to reply within a reasonable timeframe, ideally within 24 hours. Prompt responses show your commitment to customer service and increase customer satisfaction.

3. Use Professional and Courteous Language: Maintain a professional tone in all your communications. Be

polite, friendly, and respectful when addressing customer inquiries or resolving issues. Avoid using jargon or technical language that may confuse customers.

4. Provide Clear Instructions: When it comes to placing an order, making payment, or arranging for pickup or delivery, provide clear and concise instructions to your customers. Include step-by-step guidance, important dates, and any specific requirements to ensure a smooth process.

5. Leverage Multiple Communication Channels: Utilize various communication channels available on Facebook Marketplace, such as direct messaging, comments, and post updates. Choose the most appropriate channel based on the nature of the communication. Encourage customers to reach out to you if they have any questions or concerns.

6. Document Communication: Keep a record of all customer interactions and important details related to each transaction. This can be useful for reference, dispute resolution, or tracking any special requests or agreements.

By maintaining clear communication throughout the sales process, you can establish trust, provide excellent customer service, and increase customer satisfaction on Facebook Marketplace.

PROVIDE EXCELLENT CUSTOMER SERVICE

Providing excellent customer service is crucial for managing your sales effectively on Facebook Marketplace. It not only helps you retain customers but also enhances your brand reputation and generates positive word-of-mouth. Here are some strategies to provide excellent customer service:

1. Promptly Address Customer Concerns: Respond to customer inquiries, concerns, or complaints as quickly as possible. Promptly addressing their issues shows that you value their satisfaction and are committed to resolving any problems that may arise.

2. Be Polite and Professional: Maintain a polite and professional tone in all your customer interactions. Use respectful language, address customers by their names if possible, and always remain courteous, even in challenging situations. Treat every customer with empathy and understanding.

3. Go the Extra Mile: Look for opportunities to exceed customer expectations. Offer personalized recommendations, provide additional information about your products, or offer small gestures of goodwill, such as including a handwritten thank-you

note or a small discount on their next purchase. These gestures can leave a lasting impression and enhance the overall customer experience.

4. Leverage Facebook Messenger for Customer Service: Utilize Facebook Messenger as a customer service channel. Respond to messages promptly, provide accurate information, and engage in real-time conversations to address customer inquiries or concerns. This direct and immediate communication channel can enhance customer satisfaction.

5. Train Your Team: If you have a team assisting you with customer service, provide them with proper training on how to handle customer inquiries, complaints, and difficult situations. Empower your team to make decisions that benefit the customer and the business, ensuring a consistent and positive customer experience.

6. Seek Feedback and Act on It: Encourage customers to provide feedback on their experience with your business. Actively listen to their suggestions and concerns and take appropriate actions to improve your products or services. Demonstrating a willingness to listen and improve shows your commitment to customer satisfaction.

By prioritizing excellent customer service, you can build strong relationships with your customers and enhance their satisfaction and loyalty on Facebook Marketplace.

BEST PRACTICES FOR NEGOTIATING WITH BUYERS

When it comes to negotiating with buyers on Facebook Marketplace, employing effective strategies can help you achieve favorable outcomes while maintaining a positive selling experience.

Here are some best practices for negotiating with buyers:

1. Negotiate: Engage in a negotiation process rather than outright rejecting or accepting offers. Be open to discussing the price and finding a mutually agreeable solution that benefits both parties.

2. Leave the Conversation: If a buyer's offer is too low or unreasonable, it's okay to politely exit the conversation. You can simply thank them for their interest and let them know that you're considering other offers. Leaving the conversation can sometimes prompt buyers to reconsider their offer and come back with a better one.

3. Be Firm: While negotiating, maintain a firm stance on the value of your item. Clearly articulate why your price is justified, considering factors such as brand, condition, rarity, or

demand. Avoid undervaluing your item or settling for less than it's worth.

4. Accept if Desperate: If you're in a situation where you urgently need to sell an item or are willing to accept a lower price, you can consider accepting offers that may be lower than your initial asking price. However, be mindful of not consistently undervaluing your items, as it may set a precedent for future negotiations.

5. Block: If you encounter buyers who are consistently disrespectful or unreasonable in their negotiation attempts, you have the option to block them. Blocking such buyers helps maintain a positive selling environment and protects your time and energy.

6. Reason with Them: When faced with low offers, engage in a conversation with the buyer and explain why your

item is worth the price you're asking for. Highlight its unique features, quality, or any additional value it offers. Providing a reasoned explanation may help buyers understand the worth of your item and be more willing to negotiate.

7. Reach Back Out Later: If a negotiation doesn't reach a satisfactory resolution, let the buyer know that you'll consider their offer and may reach back out to them later if needed. This keeps the door open for future negotiation and allows you to reassess the situation or potentially find a different buyer.

Remember, negotiating is a skill that can be honed with practice. By adopting these best practices, you can navigate negotiations successfully and achieve favorable outcomes while selling on Facebook Marketplace.

DEALING WITH DIFFICULT CUSTOMERS

Dealing with difficult customers is a common challenge that sellers may encounter on Facebook Marketplace. It's important to handle such situations professionally and effectively to maintain a positive selling experience. Here are some tips for dealing with difficult customers:

1. Practice Reflective Listening: Listen actively to the customer's concerns and grievances. Reflect their feelings and thoughts back to them to show empathy and understanding. This can help defuse tension and create a more constructive dialogue.

2. Consider Their Affect Heuristic: Understand that customers' emotions and past experiences shape their perceptions and reactions. Put yourself in their shoes and consider how their emotions might influence

their behavior. This can help you respond in a more empathetic and understanding manner.

3. Tap into the Beginner's Mind: Approach each difficult customer interaction with a fresh perspective. Adopt a beginner's mind, free from assumptions or biases, and be open to finding solutions. This mindset can help you approach the situation with curiosity and a willingness to resolve the issue.

4. Let Go of Fear: Difficult customers can trigger feelings of defensiveness or fear. Remember to stay calm and composed, and try to detach emotionally from the situation. Responding from a place of fear or defensiveness can escalate the conflict. Instead, focus on finding a resolution.

5. "Chunk" the Problem: Break down the customer's issue into smaller,

manageable parts. Address each concern separately and work toward resolving them one by one. This approach helps you tackle the problem systematically and prevents it from feeling overwhelming.

6. Remember That Anger is Mutual: If a customer expresses anger or frustration, it's essential to remain professional and not let their emotions dictate your own. Responding with empathy and understanding can help diffuse their anger and lead to a more productive conversation.

7. Keep Calm and Carry On: Maintain a calm and composed demeanor throughout the interaction. Avoid engaging in arguments or becoming defensive. Respond professionally, sticking to the facts and focusing on finding a solution.

8. Use Your Support Resources: If a difficult customer situation escalates

or becomes unmanageable, seek support from your team or supervisor. They can provide guidance, offer additional insights, or intervene if necessary.

By applying these strategies and maintaining a professional and customer-centric approach, you can effectively handle difficult customers and turn challenging situations into positive outcomes on Facebook Marketplace.

ENSURING SAFE AND SECURE TRANSACTIONS

Ensuring safe and secure transactions is crucial when selling on Facebook Marketplace. Here are some steps that sellers can take to promote a safe and secure selling environment:

1. Conduct Transactions in Safe Locations: Choose public, well-lit

locations to meet buyers for in-person transactions. Consider meeting in a busy coffee shop, shopping center, or police station parking lot. Avoid isolated or unfamiliar locations.

2. Verify the Buyer's Identity: Before finalizing a transaction, verify the buyer's identity. Check their Facebook profile and review their ratings and reviews from previous transactions. Communicate with the buyer through the Facebook Messenger app to establish trust.

3. Set Clear Terms and Conditions: Clearly outline the terms and conditions of the sale, including the price, payment method, and any specific arrangements for shipping or pickup. Having everything in writing helps prevent misunderstandings or disputes.

4. Use Secure Payment Methods: Encourage buyers to use secure

payment methods such as PayPal, Venmo, or bank transfers. These methods offer protection against fraud and ensure that the funds are transferred securely.

5. Inspect Items before Completing the Transaction: When selling physical items, allow buyers to inspect them thoroughly before completing the transaction. This ensures that buyers are satisfied with the condition of the item and helps prevent disputes later on.

6. Trust Your Instincts: If something feels off or suspicious during the transaction process, trust your instincts and proceed with caution. If a buyer is pressuring you or offering unusual payment methods, it's best to be cautious and consider alternative buyers.

7. Protect Personal Information: Be mindful of sharing personal

information such as your address, phone number, or financial details with buyers. Use secure payment methods that don't require you to disclose sensitive information.

8. Report Suspicious Activity: If you encounter any suspicious or fraudulent activity on Facebook Marketplace, report it to Facebook immediately. This helps maintain a safe community and protects other sellers and buyers.

By following these steps and being vigilant, sellers can create a safer selling environment and minimize the risks associated with online transactions on Facebook Marketplace.

In this Chapter, we focused on managing sales and negotiations on Facebook Marketplace. We discussed various strategies and tools for effectively managing sales, including the use of CRM systems, order management tools, maintaining clear communication, and providing excellent customer service. Additionally, we provided practical tips for negotiating with buyers and handling difficult customers. Lastly, we explored steps to ensure safe and secure transactions on the platform.

Key takeaways from this chapter include:

1. Implementing CRM systems and order management tools can help streamline sales processes and improve customer relationships.

2. Clear communication and excellent customer service are essential for managing sales and building trust with customers.

3. Effective negotiation techniques, such as being firm, reasoning with buyers, and knowing when to walk away, can lead to successful transactions.

4. Dealing with difficult customers requires patience, empathy, and effective communication skills.

5. Prioritizing safety and security measures, such as meeting in public places and using secure payment methods, is crucial for a positive selling experience on Facebook Marketplace.

In the next chapter, we will delve into scaling your business on Facebook Marketplace. We will explore strategies to expand your reach, diversify your product listings, and build a brand that sets you apart from the competition. Get ready to unlock the potential for growth and take your selling endeavors on Facebook Marketplace to new heights in the upcoming chapter!

CHAPTER

SEVEN

HOW TO SCALE YOUR FACEBOOK MARKETPLACE BUSINESS

Key takeaway: This chapter focuses on strategies for scaling your Facebook Marketplace business, expanding your reach, diversifying your product listings, and building a brand.

Chapter hook: Facebook Marketplace has become a significant platform for businesses, with impressive statistics highlighting its potential. According to recent data, the average Facebook user spends 33 minutes per day on the platform, providing ample opportunities for businesses to reach a large audience. Furthermore, in 2021, Facebook Marketplace generated a staggering $26 billion in gross revenue, marking a substantial 48% increase from the previous year. These statistics demonstrate the immense potential for growth and success on Facebook Marketplace.

WHEN TO SCALE YOUR BUSINESS

Scaling your Facebook Marketplace business requires careful consideration and timing. It's essential to identify the signs that indicate your business is ready for growth and expansion. Here are some key indicators that it may be the right time to scale your business:

1. Turning down potential business/customers: If you find yourself consistently having to turn down customers or opportunities due to high demand or limited capacity, it may be a sign that your business is

ready to scale. This indicates that there is untapped market potential that you can leverage by expanding your operations.

2. Exceeding previous goals: When your business consistently surpasses its performance goals, such as revenue targets, customer acquisition metrics, or market share, it suggests that there is strong demand for your products or services. This success can be an indicator that it's time to scale and capitalize on the momentum you've built.

3. Strong cash flow and repeatable sales: A healthy cash flow and consistent, repeatable sales indicate that your business has achieved a level of stability and predictability. When you have a steady stream of revenue and a solid customer base, it provides a solid foundation for scaling your operations.

4. Proven concept and reliable infrastructure: Scaling a business requires a solid foundation. If you have a proven business concept with a market-tested product or service, and your infrastructure, systems, and processes are well-established and capable of handling increased volume, it's a good indication that you are ready to scale.

5. An atmosphere of minimal risk: Scaling a business always involves some level of risk, but if you have mitigated major risks and established contingency plans, it shows that you are prepared to take calculated risks associated with growth. Assess your market, competitors, and industry landscape to ensure that external factors are conducive to expansion.

Expanding your business prematurely can strain resources and lead to inefficiencies while scaling at the right time can propel your business to new heights. By carefully considering these signs and monitoring the health and growth of your business, you can make informed decisions about when to scale.

DIVERSIFYING YOUR PRODUCT LISTINGS

Diversifying your product offerings on Facebook Marketplace can bring several benefits to your business, including reaching a broader customer base, increasing sales opportunities, and mitigating risks associated with relying on a single product or niche. Here are key points to consider when diversifying your product listings effectively:

1. What is diversification?
   Diversification refers to expanding your product range by introducing new products or product categories

that complement your existing offerings. It involves broadening your business's scope and appealing to a wider audience.

2. Types of diversification: There are different ways to diversify your product listings. You can consider adding related products or variations of your existing products, expanding into complementary product categories, or even introducing entirely new and unrelated products.

3. Why diversify? Diversifying your product offerings can provide several benefits. It allows you to attract a broader customer base and cater to different preferences and needs. It can also help you capitalize on trends and seasonal demands, reduce dependence on a single product, and increase revenue streams.

4. Risks in diversification: While diversification offers opportunities, it

also comes with risks. Adding new products requires careful market research and assessment to ensure there is sufficient demand and profitability. It's important to consider factors such as production costs, inventory management, and marketing efforts to mitigate potential risks.

5. Examples: Look for examples of successful diversification strategies in your industry or on Facebook Marketplace. Study how other businesses have expanded their product range while maintaining a cohesive brand identity and meeting customer expectations.

6. Tips for effective diversification:

    - Conduct market research: Identify customer needs, market trends, and potential gaps in the market to guide your diversification decisions.

- Evaluate potential products: Assess the demand, profitability, and fit with your existing offerings before adding new products.

- Manage inventory and logistics: Ensure you have the capacity to handle increased inventory and fulfillment needs associated with diversification.

- Maintain brand consistency: Despite offering diverse products, maintain a consistent brand image and quality across your listings.

- Market and promote effectively: Develop targeted marketing strategies to attract customers to your diversified product listings.

- Seek customer feedback: Gather insights from your customers to understand their preferences and refine your product offerings.

By diversifying your product listings strategically, you can expand your business's reach and capture new opportunities on Facebook Marketplace. It's crucial to balance market demand, profitability, and operational capabilities to ensure a successful diversification strategy.

BUILDING A BRAND ON FACEBOOK MARKETPLACE

Building a strong brand presence on Facebook Marketplace is essential for standing out among competitors and establishing trust with your target audience. Here are key points to consider when it comes to building your brand on Facebook Marketplace:

1. Why build your brand?

   ☐ Differentiation: In a crowded marketplace where numerous

sellers offer similar products, building a strong brand helps you stand out from the competition. A well-defined brand identity and unique value proposition enable you to differentiate your business and attract customers who resonate with your brand's values, personality, and offerings.

☐ Trust and credibility: Trust is a crucial factor in any customer's decision-making process. A reputable brand instills confidence and credibility among potential buyers. When customers recognize and trust your brand, they are more likely to choose your products over competitors. Positive experiences, consistent messaging, and a professional brand image all contribute to building trust with your target audience.

☐ Customer loyalty: A strong brand fosters customer loyalty and encourages repeat purchases. When customers have a positive experience with your brand, they are more likely to develop a sense of loyalty and become brand advocates. Repeat customers not only generate ongoing revenue but can also spread positive word-of-mouth, attracting new customers to your brand.

☐ Increased visibility: Building your brand on Facebook Marketplace increases your visibility and exposure to a wider audience. By establishing a strong brand presence, you can capture the attention of potential customers who are actively browsing and searching for products. As your brand gains visibility, it becomes more recognizable, leading to increased engagement and potential conversions.

☐ Consistent brand messaging: A well-developed brand ensures that your messaging is consistent across all touchpoints. This consistency helps create a cohesive and recognizable brand identity. From your profile description and product listings to your communication with customers, maintaining a consistent brand voice and messaging enhances brand recognition and reinforces your value proposition.

☐ Brand storytelling: Building your brand on Facebook Marketplace allows you to share your unique brand story with customers. By effectively communicating your brand's mission, values, and origin, you can create an emotional connection with your target audience. Engaging storytelling helps customers relate to your brand on a deeper level, leading to stronger brand loyalty and a higher likelihood of repeat business.

- Engaging with your audience: Facebook Marketplace provides opportunities to engage with potential buyers directly. Responding to inquiries, addressing customer feedback, and providing helpful information build rapport and demonstrate your commitment to customer satisfaction. Engaging with your audience in a timely and personalized manner strengthens your brand's reputation and fosters a positive customer experience.

In conclusion, building your brand on Facebook Marketplace offers numerous advantages, including differentiation, trust and credibility, customer loyalty, increased visibility, and consistent brand messaging. By investing in your brand's presence and reputation, you can create a strong foundation for long-term success and growth on the platform.

2. Strategies for brand-building:

- Consistent branding elements: Use consistent visual elements such as logos, color schemes, and fonts across your Facebook Marketplace listings and other marketing materials.

- Compelling brand story: Craft a compelling narrative that communicates your brand's values, mission, and unique selling points to engage and resonate with your target audience.

- Engage with your audience: Respond promptly to customer inquiries, comments, and reviews to show that you value customer feedback and are committed to their satisfaction.

- Showcase customer testimonials: Encourage satisfied customers to provide testimonials or reviews, and feature them on your Facebook Marketplace page to build social proof and credibility.

- Utilize high-quality visuals: Invest in professional product photography and visually appealing content to enhance the visual representation of your brand.

- Provide excellent customer service: Deliver exceptional

customer service experiences to create positive brand associations and encourage word-of-mouth recommendations.

- Leverage Facebook features: Take advantage of Facebook's advertising tools, insights, and targeting capabilities to reach your ideal audience and build brand awareness.

- Collaborate with influencers: Partner with relevant influencers or micro-influencers who align with your brand values to expand your reach and tap into their engaged audience.

By implementing these strategies, you can establish a strong and recognizable brand presence on Facebook Marketplace, leading to increased customer trust, loyalty, and ultimately, higher sales.

In this chapter, we have focused on scaling your Facebook Marketplace business. We discussed the signs that indicate it's time to scale, such as increased demand and consistent profits. We also explored the benefits of diversifying your product listings and provided tips on how to do it effectively. Additionally, we emphasized the importance of building a brand on Facebook Marketplace and shared strategies for brand-building.

Key takeaways from this chapter:

- Recognize the signs that it's time to scale your business, including turning down potential customers, exceeding previous goals, and having a strong cash flow.

- Diversify your product listings to attract a wider range of customers and reduce dependency on a single product.

- Building a brand on Facebook Marketplace is crucial for

differentiation, trust-building, customer loyalty, and increased visibility.

- Strategies for brand-building include consistent branding elements, engaging with your audience, showcasing customer testimonials, utilizing high-quality visuals, providing excellent customer service, and leveraging Facebook's features and influencer partnerships.

In the next chapter, we will cover potential changes to the Marketplace and tips for staying ahead of the curve and adapting to changes. Get ready to take your Facebook Marketplace business to the next level in Chapter 8!

CHAPTER

EIGHT

THE FUTURE OF FACEBOOK MARKETPLACE

Chapter Hook: "'Trends come like a series of ocean waves, bringing the high tide when things are good and, as conditions recede, the low tide appears. These trends come unexpectedly, unpredictably, and they have to be weathered with temperance, poise, and patience - good or bad.'" - Jesse Lauriston Livermore

As we navigate the ever-evolving landscape of Facebook Marketplace, it is essential to stay ahead of the curve and adapt to the changes that lie ahead. In this chapter, we will explore the future of

Facebook Marketplace, discussing potential shifts, emerging trends, and strategies for maintaining a competitive edge.

POTENTIAL CHANGES TO FACEBOOK MARKETPLACE

Facebook Marketplace continues to evolve and adapt to the changing landscape of e-commerce and user preferences. In this section, we will explore some potential changes that are emerging or have been introduced by Facebook, indicating the direction in which the Marketplace is headed.

1. Reels are here to stay: With the popularity of short-form video content, Facebook has introduced Reels to compete with platforms like TikTok. Reels offer sellers an opportunity to showcase their products creatively and engage with

their audience in a more dynamic way.

2. Live FB shops: Facebook Live has gained traction as a powerful tool for sellers to showcase products in real time. By integrating live video streams with the Marketplace, sellers can create interactive shopping experiences and drive engagement.

3. Meta Verified: Facebook's rebranding to Meta emphasizes its commitment to virtual reality and the metaverse. This shift may bring new opportunities and features to Facebook Marketplace, integrating virtual experiences and immersive shopping.

4. AI-powered content creation and discovery: Facebook's advancements in artificial intelligence enable personalized content recommendations and streamlined discovery of relevant products. AI

algorithms analyze user preferences and behavior, enhancing the shopping experience on the Marketplace.

5. Simplified campaign and targeting with AI: AI-powered tools facilitate more effective advertising campaigns on Facebook Marketplace. Automated targeting and optimization algorithms help sellers reach their desired audience and maximize the impact of their ads.

6. More opportunities for growth: Facebook Marketplace continues to expand globally, opening doors for sellers to reach a wider audience. As the platform gains popularity and user adoption increases, there are increased opportunities for business growth.

7. Chatbots as customer support: Chatbots are increasingly being used to provide customer support on Facebook Marketplace. They can assist with inquiries, provide quick

responses, and offer personalized recommendations, enhancing the overall customer experience.

8. Easier discovery of groups and communities: Facebook has made improvements to the discovery of groups and communities, allowing sellers to find niche communities that align with their target audience. Joining relevant groups can help businesses connect with potential customers and establish their brand presence.

By staying informed about these potential changes and leveraging the latest features and tools offered by Facebook, sellers on the Marketplace can adapt their strategies and stay ahead of the competition.

STAYING AHEAD OF THE CURVE

To stay ahead of changes and trends in the Facebook Marketplace, it's important to be proactive and adaptive in your approach. Here are some general and specific tips to help you stay ahead of the curve:

General Tips:

1. Stay informed: Continuously educate yourself about the latest trends and developments in the e-commerce industry. Subscribe to relevant newsletters, follow industry experts and influencers, and attend webinars or conferences to stay updated.

2. Monitor competitor activity: Keep an eye on what your competitors are doing on Facebook Marketplace and other platforms. Analyze their strategies, pricing, product offerings, and customer engagement to identify potential opportunities or gaps in the market.

3. Embrace data-driven decision-making: Utilize analytics tools to gather insights about your customers, their preferences, and purchasing behavior. Data-driven decision-making allows you to optimize your strategies, identify areas for improvement, and capitalize on emerging trends.

4. Engage with your audience: Actively engage with your customers and potential buyers on Facebook Marketplace. Respond to messages and comments promptly, address their concerns, and seek feedback to understand their needs better. Building strong relationships with your audience can help you stay attuned to their changing preferences.

5. Stay adaptable: Embrace change and be willing to adapt your strategies and tactics as the marketplace evolves. Be open to experimenting with new features, technologies, and marketing

approaches to remain relevant and competitive.

Specific Tips for Facebook Marketplace:

1. Explore new features: Facebook frequently introduces new features and tools on the Marketplace. Keep abreast of these updates and explore how you can leverage them to enhance your listings, improve visibility, and engage with your audience effectively.

2. Utilize targeted advertising: Facebook offers robust advertising options to target specific audiences. Stay updated with the latest advertising features and best practices to optimize your campaigns and reach the right customers.

3. Leverage Facebook groups: Engage with Facebook groups that align with your target audience and industry. Participate in discussions, offer valuable insights, and share relevant

content. This can help you build a reputation, establish your brand presence, and generate leads.

4. Embrace visual content: Visual content is highly engaging and can attract more attention on Facebook Marketplace. Invest in high-quality product images and videos that highlight your offerings and showcase their unique features.

5. Build customer trust: Prioritize building trust with your customers on the platform. Encourage and respond to customer reviews, provide excellent customer service, and maintain transparency in your transactions. Positive reviews and satisfied customers can enhance your reputation and attract more buyers.

By following these general and specific tips, you can position yourself for success on Facebook Marketplace and stay ahead of the curve in the ever-evolving e-commerce landscape.

ADAPTING TO CHANGES IN THE MARKETPLACE

In a rapidly changing marketplace, sellers need to stay flexible and adapt to new trends and dynamics to remain competitive. Here are some strategies to help you navigate and adapt to changes effectively:

1. Start with a customer focus: Keep your customers at the center of your decision-making process. Continuously gather feedback, conduct market research, and stay attuned to their changing needs and preferences. By understanding your customers, you can adapt your offerings and strategies to meet their evolving demands.

2. Recognize early warning signs of change: Stay vigilant and be proactive

in identifying early warning signs of shifts in the marketplace. Monitor industry trends, consumer behavior, and emerging technologies. Being aware of these changes early on allows you to anticipate and adapt to them before they have a significant impact on your business.

3. Monitor the competition with an innovative mindset: Keep a close eye on your competitors and their strategies. Identify innovative approaches they are implementing and assess their effectiveness. This insight can inspire new ideas and help you differentiate your business. Embrace a mindset of continuous improvement and be willing to innovate and experiment.

4. Identify strengths and gap areas in your team: Assess the skills and capabilities of your team members to identify areas of strength and areas that may require development. As the

marketplace evolves, your team needs to have the necessary skills and knowledge to adapt. Provide training and resources to fill any skill gaps and encourage a culture of learning and professional development.

5. Schedule regular training of staff: Continuously invest in the training and development of your staff. Provide them with the tools and knowledge they need to navigate changes in the marketplace effectively. This can include training on new technologies, sales techniques, customer service, or any other areas relevant to your business.

6. Create and practice a culture of agility: Foster a culture of agility within your organization. Encourage open communication, collaboration, and adaptability. Embrace change as an opportunity for growth and improvement. When everyone in the organization is adaptable and open to

change, it becomes easier to pivot and respond to market dynamics.

By following these strategies and remaining flexible, you can position your business to adapt and thrive in an ever-changing marketplace.

In this chapter, we discussed the importance of staying ahead of changes in the Facebook Marketplace and provided tips on how to adapt and thrive in an evolving marketplace environment. We explored potential changes that could impact your selling experience and strategies to stay proactive and agile in the face of those changes. By staying informed and adaptable, you can maintain a competitive edge and maximize your success on Facebook Marketplace.

Key Takeaways:

1. Stay informed: Keep yourself updated with the latest news and announcements regarding Facebook Marketplace. Follow official Facebook channels, join relevant

groups or forums, and stay connected with other sellers to gain insights into upcoming changes and updates.

2. Adaptability is key: Understand that change is inevitable, and the marketplace landscape can evolve rapidly. Be open to adapting your strategies, processes, and listings to align with new features, policies, or trends on Facebook Marketplace.

3. Embrace new features: Facebook frequently introduces new features and tools to enhance the selling experience. Stay proactive and explore these features to leverage them to your advantage. For example, consider utilizing promotional tools, improved messaging features, or additional selling options offered by Facebook.

4. Optimize your listings: Continuously optimize your listings to align with changes in algorithms, search

algorithms, and buyer preferences. Regularly review your descriptions, titles, keywords, and images to ensure they are in line with current best practices and trends.

5. Solicit and adapt to feedback: Pay attention to feedback from buyers and adapt accordingly. Feedback can provide valuable insights into areas where you can improve your listings, customer service, or overall selling experience.

6. Build relationships: Cultivate relationships with other sellers, buyers, and influencers within the Facebook Marketplace community. Engage in discussions, share insights, and collaborate to gain knowledge, stay updated, and build a strong network.

7. Experiment and iterate: Don't be afraid to experiment with different strategies, tactics, or approaches. Test

new listing formats, pricing models, or marketing techniques to see what works best for your specific niche and target audience.

By implementing these tips and approaches, you can position yourself to adapt to changes and navigate the evolving landscape of Facebook Marketplace successfully.

SUMMARY OF ALL THE CHAPTERS

Chapter 1: Introduction to Facebook Marketplace. In this chapter, we explored the basics of Facebook Marketplace and its immense potential for sellers. We discussed the benefits of selling on the platform, how to set up a seller account, and the key features and functionalities of Facebook Marketplace. Remember, by leveraging the power of Facebook Marketplace, you can tap into a vast audience and unlock new opportunities for your business.

Chapter 2: We discussed setting up your Facebook Marketplace account, understanding the dashboard, and personalizing your profile.

Chapter 3: Creating Compelling Product Listings. In this chapter, we explored the art of creating compelling product listings on Facebook Marketplace. We discussed the key elements of a persuasive listing, such as high-quality visuals, clear and descriptive product descriptions, competitive pricing, and accurate categorization. By optimizing your listings, you can attract more potential buyers and increase your chances of making sales.

Chapter 4: We discussed various marketing techniques to enhance sales on Facebook Marketplace. We also discussed the importance of effective communication, leveraging Facebook Ads, optimizing for search engine visibility, and utilizing social proof to build trust and credibility.

Chapter 5: We delved into the fascinating world of Facebook Marketplace and explored the most commonly sold items on the platform. We also discussed top-selling items on Facebook Marketplace and why they sell.

Chapter 6: Managing Sales Effectively. Managing your sales effectively is vital for maintaining customer satisfaction and growing your business. We discussed tips for order management, clear communication with customers, providing excellent customer service, and ensuring safe and secure transactions. By implementing these practices, you can streamline your sales processes, build trust with customers, and enhance their overall experience.

Chapter 7: How to Scale Your Facebook Marketplace Business. In this chapter, we explored strategies for scaling your business on Facebook Marketplace. We discussed signs that indicate it's time to scale, the benefits of diversifying your product listings, and building a brand on the platform. By expanding your reach, diversifying your offerings, and establishing a strong brand presence, you can unlock new growth opportunities and elevate your business to the next level.

Chapter 8: The Future of Facebook Marketplace. The final chapter delved into the future of Facebook Marketplace and how sellers can stay ahead of the curve. We discussed potential changes to the platform, staying updated on trends, and adapting to marketplace dynamics. By embracing change, monitoring competition, and staying customer-focused, you can position your business for success in the evolving landscape of Facebook Marketplace.

Congratulations on completing this book and gaining valuable insights into selling on Facebook Marketplace! You have learned how to leverage the platform to reach a wide audience, understand and engage with your target market, create compelling listings, optimize visibility, set competitive prices, manage sales effectively, and prepare for the future. Armed with this knowledge, you are well-equipped to take your Facebook Marketplace business to new heights.

Remember, success on Facebook Marketplace requires continuous learning, adaptation, and a customer-centric approach. Keep refining your strategies, exploring new opportunities, and staying ahead of the curve. The future is bright, and with the lessons learned from this book, you are on your way to achieving greater success in your selling endeavors on Facebook Marketplace.

Thanks!

CONCLUSION

Congratulations on reaching the conclusion of this book on selling on Facebook Marketplace! Throughout these chapters, we have explored the ins and outs of leveraging this powerful platform to grow your business and reach a wider audience. Now, let's recap the key takeaways and set you up for success.

In Chapter 1, we introduced you to the world of Facebook Marketplace and its immense potential for sellers like you. By tapping into the vast user base and the platform's features, you can unlock new opportunities and expand your business.

In Chapter 2, we taught you how to set up your Facebook Marketplace account, understand the dashboard, and personalize your profile.

Creating compelling product listings was the focus of Chapter Three. We discussed the key elements of a persuasive listing, from high-quality visuals to clear descriptions and competitive pricing. By optimizing your listings, you can attract more potential buyers and increase your chances of making sales.

Marketing techniques to enhance sales on Facebook Marketplace was our focus in Chapter Four. We also discussed the importance of effective communication, leveraging Facebook Ads, optimizing for search engine visibility, and utilizing social proof to build trust and credibility.

In Chapter 5, we delved into the fascinating world of Facebook Marketplace and explored the most commonly sold items on the platform. We also discussed top-selling items on Facebook Marketplace and why they sell.

Managing your sales effectively was the focus of Chapter 6. We discussed tips for order management, clear communication with customers, providing excellent customer service, and ensuring safe and secure transactions. By implementing these practices, you can streamline your sales processes and build trust with your customers.

Chapter 7 explored strategies for scaling your business on Facebook Marketplace. We discussed signs that indicate it's time to scale, the benefits of diversifying your product listings, and building a brand on the platform. These strategies will help you unlock new growth opportunities and elevate your business to the next level.

In the final chapter, we discussed the future of Facebook Marketplace and how to stay ahead of the curve. By embracing change, monitoring competition, and staying customer-focused, you can position your business for success in the evolving landscape of Facebook Marketplace.

As you close this book, remember that success on Facebook Marketplace requires continuous learning, adaptation, and a customer-centric approach. Refine your strategies, explore new opportunities, and stay ahead of the curve. The future is bright, and with the lessons learned from this book, you are well-equipped to achieve greater success in your selling endeavors.

I want to leave you a personal note. Selling on Facebook Marketplace is not just about making transactions; it's about building connections, creating value, and enjoying the benefits of your hard work. As an author, I have witnessed success stories of individuals and businesses who have thrived on this platform. Now, it's your turn.

I encourage you to take advantage of the opportunities presented by Facebook Marketplace. Set your business up for success, embrace the journey, and enjoy the rewards that come with it. Remember, you have the knowledge and tools to make a significant impact.

Before we part ways, I kindly ask you to leave a review on Amazon. Your feedback will not only help me as an author but also guide other readers in their journey to succeed on Facebook Marketplace.

Thank you for choosing this book and investing your time and energy into learning and growing. I wish you the best of luck on your journey. May your business thrive, and your dreams become a reality.

Warm regards,

- Jeff

REFERENCES AND CITATIONS

Reference:

Title: "The Facebook Effect: The Inside Story of the Company That Is Connecting the World"

Author: David Kirkpatrick

Year: 2010

Publisher: Simon & Schuster

Citation:

Kirkpatrick, D. (2010). "The Facebook Effect: The Inside Story of the Company That Is Connecting the World." Simon & Schuster.

Reference:

Title: "Social Media Marketing All-in-One For Dummies"

Authors: Jan Zimmerman, Deborah Ng

Year: 2017

Publisher: For Dummies

Citation:

Zimmerman, J., & Ng, D. (2017). "Social Media Marketing All-in-One For Dummies." For Dummies.

Reference:

Title: "Facebook Marketing: An Hour a Day"

Authors: Chris Treadaway, Mari Smith

Year: 2012

Publisher: Sybex

Citation:

Treadaway, C., & Smith, M. (2012). "Facebook Marketing: An Hour a Day." Sybex.

Title: "Ultimate Guide to Facebook Advertising: How to Access 1 Billion Potential Customers in 10 Minutes"

Authors: Perry Marshall, Keith Krance, Thomas Meloche

Year: 2018

Publisher: Entrepreneur Press

Citation:

Marshall, P., Krance, K., & Meloche, T. (2018). "Ultimate Guide to Facebook Advertising: How to Access 1 Billion Potential Customers in 10 Minutes." Entrepreneur Press.

Reference:

Title: "The Art of Social Media: Power Tips for Power Users"

Authors: Guy Kawasaki, Peg Fitzpatrick

Year: 2014

Publisher: Portfolio

Citation:

Kawasaki, G., & Fitzpatrick, P. (2014). "The Art of Social Media: Power Tips for Power Users." Portfolio.

Printed in Great Britain
by Amazon